Sustainable Tourism:

A Small Business Handbook for Success **‹**

Pamela Lanier

Author: Pamela Lanier
Editor: Laurence Blanchette Hamel
Compositor: John Richards
Cover Design and Design Devices: Inga Vesik

1st ed. June 2013

Copyright 2013 EcoGo.org

Distributed by CreateSpace, Amazon, Baker & Taylor, Ingram, and in bookstores everywhere!

Published by EcoGo.org, Sonoma, California

info@EcoGo.org

ISBN: 978-1489542236

Contents

i

Acknowledgements

WE WOULD LIKE TO EXTEND OUR DEEPEST THANKS TO OUR
dedicated team of interns, Ryath Beauchamp, Sean Callahan, Beverly
Hammond, David McClelland, Anna-Brit Schlaepfer, Jessica Shoemaker,
without whose sharp minds, time and effort we would not have been able to
complete this project. A special thanks to Laurence Blanchette, Senior Editor,
whose organization and leadership helped bring this book to life.

An honest "thank you!" to our contributing authors, Patty Apple, Sylvia
Bernstein, Hector Ceballos-Lascurain, Kristin Coates, Kathleen Harrison,
Candi Horton, Dan Linsky, Amanda Mayhew, and Stanley Selengut, whose
expertise is truly appreciated.

To the eight properties featured in this book (Bardessono, Camp Denali,
Concordia, Ecoventura, Guludo Beach Resort, Inn Serendipity, Lapa Rios,
and Los Poblanos), thank you for allowing us to study and analyze your
best practices in conservation, sustainable development, and community
involvement. We have made every effort to accurately portray your property.
We will happily rectify any errors or omissions in future issues of this book,
on our website, and in any other future publications.

Warm thanks to Elena Garnache and her students for contributing to our
project with a beautiful and heartfelt collage poster titled "Our Planet. Our
Future." Your vision of a greener tomorrow is an inspiration to us all.

Thanks also to Robert L. Biggs, John Richards, Inga Vesik, Susan Heeringa-
Pieper, Professor Robert Girling, Jim Kuhns, Michael McCloskey, Clara
Valdes, Oren Wool, Eve Muir, Cree McCree, Kenji Williams, Kathy Pine,
Ed Begley Jr., Bryan Welch, Roohi Moola, Doug McConnell, Richard Dale,
and Bernie Krause, for your professional and emotional support during the
development stages of this project.

ii

About this book

THIS HANDBOOK IS INTENDED TO BE USED BY SMALL AND MEDIUM
businesses, entrepreneurs and organizations in the tourism industry as a
resource and guide to adopt specific actions to become more sustainable.
Best practices and critical components are discussed and supported by case
studies and supplemental articles, providing an easy-to-digest format meant
to enable you to carry out key development steps for a sustainable future.

The book can be read in its entirety, but is also designed for each chapter
to stand alone. This allows readers with a specific goal in mind to jump right
into the appropriate section with confidence, knowing that all necessary
information and tools will be provided.

Dive deeper into any topic covered in this book by visiting the resource
section. Organized by chapter, this list of supplemental readings allows you
to easily find more information on the topic of your interest.

iii

Introduction by
Stanley Selengut

FROM MAHO BAY'S INCEPTION IN 1974, WE HAVE REMAINED TRUE to the guiding principles illustrated in the following pages. Ideas such as exposing guests to an authentic sense of place. That is choreographing the indigenous architectures, food, music, dance, plants, animals, cultures, folk art, customs and contact with local people into a unique experience.

Also sustainability: taking the long-term responsibility for the well-being of the land you are working on and the communities around it. Programs such as feral animal control, wildlife management, native plant landscaping, recycling, solar design, conservation, local economic development, training and fair employment policies.

Also important is the interpretation and education of gusts. Hopefully, every visitor will return home with a stronger appreciation of nature and the knowledge of how better to live within the earth's renewable resources.

I encourage you to read on and may your efforts be as rewarding as mine have been.

1

Understanding Ecotourism

TOURISM IS ACCOUNTING FOR AN INCREASING PORTION OF THE world economy. According to the World Travel and Tourism Council, in 2011 alone, travel and tourism made up 9% of GDP, employed 250 million around the world, and boasted a profit of 6 trillion USD.[1] As such a significant component economic activity, travel and tourism have the potential to make a significant impact on the world. We propose tipping the balance in favor of making a positive impact on the world, and we will explore the economic, social, and environmental benefits of ecotourism.

Ecotourism, as defined by IUCN, is "environmentally responsible travel and visitation to relatively undisturbed natural areas, in order to enjoy and appreciate nature (and any accompanying cultural features—both past and present) that promotes conservation, has low visitor impact, and provides for beneficially active socio-economic involvement of local populations"[2]. Ecotourism is an effective way for businesses in a tourism destination to have a positive impact on their host community. Whether the business at stake is a conservation organization, a lodging facility, a product-based company,

---

1 *World Travel & Tourism Council, Benchmarking Travel & Tourism, Americas Summary: How does Travel & Tourism compare to other sectors?* April, 2012.
2 International Union for Conservation of Nature, www.iucn.org.

a service provider, or anything in between, ecotourism provides the proper guidelines for sustainable and responsible business practices that promote the preservation of natural resources and wildlife and contribute to the socio-cultural and economic growth of the local community.

With the principles of ecotourism in mind, it is possible to devise a business model that promotes and protects the environment and local community. In order to successfully embody ecotourism, businesses need to consider the following three measures: Sustainable Business Practices, Community Development and Environmental Stewardship. Sustainable business practices are the steps that a business takes to minimize its environmental impacts and maximize its self-sufficiency, which includes building material selection, energy choices, waste management, and water usage. Community development entails the social, cultural and economic effects that the business and its visitors have on the local inhabitants. Not only should local culture, traditions and values always be respected while running a business, but there should also be a commitment to supporting and strengthening the local community. Environmental stewardship is the activities and experiences made available to visitors that allow them to discover and appreciate the beauty of the natural environment and wildlife. Arts and crafts featuring local and sustainable materials, hiking, cooking classes, and canoeing are only a few examples of activities that allow visitors to delve into the destination and engage with the environment. This can also include encouraging visitors to partake in local volunteer preservation or conservation projects, either physically or financially. By placing these three pillars as the supporting blocks of any tourism-related operation, businesses can promote environmental, social and economic sustainability and have a lasting positive impact on the host community.

Ecotourism—The "Buzz" Words

By Amanda Mayhew

As the negative impacts resulting from years of unfettered use of the earth's natural resources have compounded and grown visible to the general public, the call for a more hands-on sustainable approach to resource management and preservation has emerged. Tourism, as one of the world's dominant economic sectors, has enormous natural, cultural, and social impacts on a global scale.

Ecotourism—The "Buzz" Words

cont'd.

The potential for these impacts to do harm is ever present, but there is equal potential for the impacts of the industry to be positive. Ecotourism, a sustainable alternative to conventional tourism, refers to the notion of balancing tourism development with the protection of the developed area's natural and cultural resources. When practiced correctly, ecotourism serves to not only minimize potential negative impacts but also to promote education and conservation of our world's precious biodiversity.

Unfortunately, as terms such as 'eco' and 'green' have become buzzwords, many unscrupulous tourism operators are exploiting the 'eco' label in order to boost marketing potential for the sole purpose of economic gain. This process, referred to as greenwashing (the act of misleading consumers in regard to a business's environmental practices, products, and services and adherence to accepted standards) is a growing problem for ecotourism. True ecotourism operations suffer as false ecotourism practitioners damage the credibility of the industry as a whole.

What is it?

The International Ecotourism Society (TIES) defines ecotourism as: "responsible travel to natural areas that conserves the environment and improves the welfare of local people." Though various definitions exist, the underlying principles of ecotourism remain the same.

Ecotourism:

- Minimizes impact
- Uses environmental education (interpretation) to build environmental and cultural awareness and respect
- Uses ecologically sustainable operations and management
- Provides positive experiences for both visitors and hosts
- Provides direct support and financial benefits for nature conservation

cont'd.

Ecotourism—The "Buzz" Words

- Uses ecologically sustainable operations and management
- Provides positive experiences for both visitors and hosts
- Provides direct support and financial benefits for nature conservation
- Provides economic benefits and empowerment for local people

CONservation:

unscrupulous ecotourism operations ("con men") that practice the act of greenwashing, or falsely claiming that their businesses or attractions contribute to conservation and adhere to the principles of ecotourism.

What you should know

In order to avoid falling victim to CONservation, it is important to first understand that different classifications of 'green' or 'sustainable' tourism exist, and how to differentiate between them. For example:

- *Green tourism:* A general term for environmentally friendly tourism intended to reduce costs and maximize benefits.
- *Nature-based tourism:* A general term for a tourism activity or experience that occurs in natural areas.
- *Ecotourism:* A type of nature-based tourism consisting of responsible travel in natural areas that promotes conservation and education.

Ecotourism—The "Buzz" Words

cont'd.

Ecotourism experiences should:

- Incorporate environmental learning (knowledge, understanding)
- Facilitate changes in environmental attitudes and behaviors
- Move ecotourists from a passive role (nature-based recreation) to a more active role, where the activities of ecotourists (both on and off-site) contribute to the health and viability of the environment.

What you can do

- When planning your next eco-adventure, use the checklist below to ensure that you are receiving a genuine ecotourism experience and not falling victim to CONservation!

Does your ecotourism experience:

- Minimize impact?
- Use environmental education (interpretation)?
- Build environmental and cultural awareness and respect?
- Use ecologically sustainable operations and management?
- Provide positive experiences for both visitors and hosts?
- Provide direct support and financial benefits for nature conservation?
- Provide economic benefits and empowerment for local people?
- Don't be afraid to ask your ecotourism provider:
- Do they have a written policy or certification from a reputable ecotourism certification scheme?
- What, specifically, have they done to help protect the environment and support conservation?

cont'd.

Ecotourism—The "Buzz" Words

- How do they measure their contribution to conservation and local communities?
- How many local people do they employ?
- Do they provide information to tourists on local cultures and customs?
- Do they educate tourists on local fauna and flora?
- How can you get involved with local conservation efforts during your stay?

Amanda Mayhew is an ecotourism specialist.

2

Sustainable Business: Building and Operating Your Business

WHEN CREATING AN ECOTOURISM FACILITY AND BUSINESS MODEL, green initiatives should be implemented at every stage of the building and management processes. The overarching goals are to minimize the impact on the environment and maximize self-sufficiency. With these two standards in mind, an eco-tourism center can be created that aesthetically complements the surrounding area, is respectful and beneficial to the local community, minimizes energy requirements, and creates a closed-loop waste system.

MINIMIZING ENVIRONMENTAL IMPACTS

The primary goal when constructing a new structure or making an existing structure your own is to create a net positive effect on the local environment. Minimizing your impact on your natural surroundings is a key component of preserving and conserving the beauty of the pristine surroundings that attracts tourists and travelers in the first place.

Every business decision must consider the impacts and repercussions it may have on the environment. From selecting a site location to selecting building materials and designing the interior, every step of the process needs to factor in the environment.

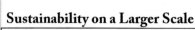

Sustainability on a Larger Scale

FOSTI Gets an Inside Look at Kimpton Hotels

Greening an existing business or establishing a new green business can seem like a daunting project. After all, there are so many environmental considerations and product choices that it can all be very overwhelming. Friends of Sustainable Tourism International (FOSTI) has a goal to provide business owners, entrepreneurs, organizations, and other thought leaders with the resources necessary to implement environmentally conscious business decisions and projects.

Take Kimpton Hotels, for example. According to Steve Pinetti, Senior VP Inspiration & Creativity, this hospitality provider has had a green outlook on running a business right from the beginning. Recycling has been part of daily operation since 1981, and meals were comprised of organic ingredients long before it became trendy. Bedford Hotel and Cafe had a big organic garden on the back deck and had a rack of shelves filled with plants and herbs.

As with many things in life, being a green hotel is an ongoing project. As new technologies and products enter the marketplace, businesses and organizations need to be flexible and optimize the latest offerings. Kimpton Hotels has been a poster child when it comes to continual improvements in the green direction. Where ever possible, sustainable products replaced their traditional counterparts, including changes like efficient light bulbs, cardboard compacting, non-toxic and environmentally friendly cleaning supplies, etc. Despite the common trend of leaving lights on in unused rooms, Kimpton began significantly reducing their power usage by turning out the lights.

cont'd.

Sustainability on a Larger Scale

In 1995, Kimpton Hotels was the first to put in an Eco floor at one of their hotels. Hotel Triton featured an entire level of environmentally conscious guestrooms that boasted organic foods in their mini bar, first generation LED lights, recycled paper, soy ink for printers, eco-friendly linens and terry, and eco-friendly bathroom amenities such as biodegradable mini bottles. The California EPA (Environmental Protection Agency) identified Triton as the model hotel for the state of California to encourage sustainability in the hospitality field.

In early 2005, Kimpton Hotels formalized their environmental efforts across all their properties and named the program Earth Care. Thus, all the subsequent practices became the way of life at Kimpton. The Earth Care program was a timely initiative that took place right around the time that the influential movie, Inconvenient Truth, was released. Kimpton received a lot of exposure because their immediate reaction to the movie was to increase the behavioral changes aimed at diminishing their carbon footprint. By comparison, many hospitality companies responded simply by writing a carbon offset check and not changing their behaviors, products or practices.

For Kimpton Hotels, embodying environmental consciousness and promoting a small footprint lifestyle came as an extension of personal standards. The fact that founder, Bill Kimpton, had a high level of environmental consciousness made this effort part of the way of life from the beginning. There were few implementation challenges because employees were selected based on a shared value system that included caring for the Earth. Kimpton seeks individuals who are environmentally aware and have a huge heart and desire to make the world a better place. Seeking support for new initiatives was driven by employees volunteering to research and test new products and practices, and then championing for implementation accordingly.

Sustainability on a Larger Scale

cont'd.

Today, Kimpton Hotels is comprised of 59 hotels and 64 restaurants, and there are over 140 actions taken to minimize the each property's environmental impacts, including the following:

Home Office Materials & Procedures

- Company, hotel and restaurant collateral printed on post-consumer recycled content paper
- Company and hotel collateral printed using soy based inks
- Established national office product partnership with Staples, recognized leader in the industry for ecological responsibility
- Created EarthCare performance tracking and monitoring system to ensure consistent progress
- HR Benefits document put online: 150,000 pages saved—50 page doc, sent to 3,000 employees
- Printed Kimpton annual report only by request—report published online
- Law firms/legal council requested to send documents online and all printed materials to be double sided
- Paper expense reports eliminated—online system established
- Phone books/religious books by request policy—includes guest signage
- Hotel key cards made with eco-friendly material (30% post consumer recycled plastic)
- All new fitness floors made with recycled rubber
- Certified towels and linens through Oeko-Tex 100 Standard
- Kimpton standard "Green" building guidelines established
- EarthCare educational and training video for back of house staff (designed increase effectiveness in all areas, from recycling to following towel/linen reuse policy)

Sustainability on a Larger Scale

cont'd.

- Eco-friendly meeting program and standards
- Employee Education Initiatives
- EarthCare educational and training video for back of house staff (increased effectiveness in all areas, from recycling to following towel/linen reuse policy)
- Established EarthCare champions team of over 80 employees that support and build the EarthCare program, including a local champion at every hotel and restaurant
- Announcements, tips, and information distributed weekly to all employees about ecologically responsible issues

Hotel EarthCare Standards

Paper

- All hotel in-room materials and bills are printed on recycled post consumer copy paper (EPA minimum or greater)
- All centralized printers set to double-sided default printing, where duplex printing is available
- Phone book "by-request" policy implemented, eliminating phone books from all guest rooms
- Check out envelopes offered by request only

Water

- Implementation of water-efficient shower heads
- Implementation of water-efficient faucets
- Implementation of water-efficient toilets
- Above water efficient products are audited to ensure water efficient apparatus and products remain in place and functioning

Sustainability on a Larger Scale

cont'd.

Energy

- Implementation of energy efficient T8 and/or T5 fluorescent lighting in back of house areas
- Implementation of motion sensors in low occupancy storage areas
- Implementation of LED lights on all exit signs
- Check-in policy: maximum of one light and radio on only
- All guest rooms have CFL lighting (not available in hotels using dimmable/3-way bulbs)
- Hallway lighting 100% energy efficient lighting—CFLs and/or LEDs (where dimmable lights are not in use)

Waste Management

- In-room recycling bins (First boutique hotel group to include these bins)
- Hotel-wide recycling of cardboard
- Hotel-wide recycling of paper
- Hotel-wide recycling of glass (where municipal services available)
- Hotel-wide recycling of cans (where municipal services available)
- Hotel-wide recycling of plastic (where municipal services available)
- Recycling of batteries
- Recycling of cell phones
- Recycling of computers and peripherals
- Recycling of in-room electronics televisions, DVDs, and radios
- Donating partially-used shampoos and conditioners to local charities
- Donating used linens and towels to local charities and/or businesses

Sustainability on a Larger Scale

cont'd.

- Providing washable/reusable mugs during morning coffee service
- Providing washable/reusable mugs and glasses in back of house break rooms
- Towel reuse option encouraged through signage and eco-benefit explanation
- Linen reuse option encouraged through signage and eco-benefit explanation
- Recycling uniform and dry cleaning coat hangers back to dry cleaning company
- Recycling ink and toner cartridges
- Eco friendly hair dryer bags, where hair dryer bags are in use
- Honor bar bottled water program—water exclusively US sourced
- Recycling bins in place at business centers, meeting rooms, and fitness centers (newspaper and bottled water recycling)
- Recycling boxes/bins at all employee work stations
- Toilet paper wraps replaced with stickers (such as Palomar "P") or twine wrap
- C-Fold towels made with recycled content for public and employee restrooms (where C-Folds are used)

Toxics

- Guest room soaps use natural ingredients and come from environmentally responsible companies
- Guest room shampoos use natural ingredients and come from environmentally responsible companies
- Guest room conditioners use natural ingredients and come from environmentally responsible companies
- Low/No VOC Paints for back of house areas
- Carpet cleaning uses non-toxic and low VOC chemicals

Sustainability on a Larger Scale

cont'd.

- Spot carpet cleaning uses non-toxic product
- Break room napkins are unbleached and/or made with recycled content

Organic Products

- Use of organic and/or shade grown coffee where complimentary lobby coffee is available
- Use of organic teas where complimentary lobby tea service is available
- Organic wine served during select months during Kimpton's complimentary wine hours
- Organic food products in every honor bar
- Organic beverage product in every honor bar
- All in-room coffee is organic (where in-room coffee is available)

Other Hotel Behaviors

- Organized and hosted day long sustainability event that was open to the public—"Come Get Dirty with Us"
- Established partnership with environmentally minded organizations
- Only hotel exhibitor at San Francisco and Washington DC Green Festivals
- First hotel group partner of Recyclebank
- Initiated company wide educational and environmental EarthCare contest
- Integrated EarthCare standards into all pre-opening guidelines and training to establish ecological responsibility from day one of hotel openings
- EarthCare program description and signage displayed publicly during select times of the year
- Organic/shade grown coffee signage is in place where complimentary morning coffee is served
- Executive Management Team EarthCare plans established

cont'd.

Sustainability on a Larger Scale

- Suppliers required to submit environmental program information as part of Accounts Payable process
- All Kimpton's uniforms are created by Cintas. Cintas supports our EarthCare mission by making many of their garments with recycled polyester produced entirely from post consumer waste. This process reduces water usage and uses less energy compared to the manufacturing of polyester fiber.
- The Kimpton's Pillow Standard is naturally "green" in that it has a down/feather fill: 50% White Goose Down, 50% White Goose Feather, and 100% Cotton ticking, thread and piping, all of which are natural and biodegradable.

Additional Actions Taken by Individual Hotels and Restaurants

The practices below have been enacted by individual Kimpton hotels and restaurants and are being considered as national standards.

Paper

- Stamps used instead of paper for room charge adjustments
- C-Fold towels made with 40% recycled content
- Line staff C-Fold towels made with recycled content
- Unbleached napkins used for to-go and "doggie bag" orders
- Public restrooms offer washable/reusable hand towels
- Toilet paper made with 100% recycled content toilet paper

Water

- Restaurants eliminated bottled water through high tech on-site water filtration system

Energy

- Infrared occupancy/motion sensors to control guest room HVAC
- Energy efficient fitness equipment

Sustainability on a Larger Scale

cont'd.

- Light powered candles using rechargeable batteries
- Reuse of restaurant oil into fryer oil
- Restaurant dining areas use LED and CFL lights

Waste Management

- No individually packaged condiments such as ketchup, mustard, cream cheese, butter and preserves
- Purchase of recycled office furniture
- Preferred purchasing policy for office products made with recycled content
- Biodegradable ware used for to-go and "doggie bag" orders
- Reusable and washable laundry bags

Clean Air

- Carbon offset program addressing hotel's energy use and carbon emissions
- Carbon offset program addressing carbon emissions from management's commuting
- Complimentary and discounted hybrid parking programs
- Use of low/no VOC paints throughout the hotel or restaurant

Toxics

- Eco-friendly (PERC free) dry cleaning service
- Public restrooms use eco-friendly soaps
- Enzyme kitchen drain cleaner
- Restaurant use of eco-friendly cleaning chemicals

Organic Products

- On-site organic gardens as produce source
- 100% organic coffees and teas served at restaurants
- Organic wine available by the bottle and by the glass
- Organic beer served during select wine/beer hour

With the right resources, proper planning, and an everlasting environmental consciousness, all businesses can reduce their environmental footprint and increase their sustainability.

SITE LOCATION

Selecting an appropriate site location for an ecotourism accommodation is the first, and perhaps most critical, step towards creating an environmental attraction. Given that most ecotourism operations are located in natural areas that may be fragile or delicate, substantial consideration must be given to the planning and building of such establishments. To ensure that facilities are designed in a way that minimizes environmental impact while maximizing self-sufficiency, knowledge of the characteristics of the specific environment must be obtained. Each site is accompanied by a unique set of physical features, natural resources and attractions, and potential environmental threats, which must be considered when examining a potential site location.

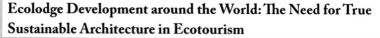

Ecolodge Development around the World: The Need for True Sustainable Architecture in Ecotourism

by Arq. Hector Ceballos-Lascurain

SITE PLANNING

Site planning and design is a process that involves in an integrated way the issues of land use, human circulation, structures, facilities and utilities within the natural and human environment. In order to ensure harmony between tourism developments and environmental protection, it is indispensable to apply sensitive design of infrastructure, master site planning, ecologically and socially conscious site design, and landscaping.

Preserving the special characteristics of a tourism destination demands an in-depth understanding of the natural systems on the site, as well as an immersion into the time-tested cultural responses to that environment's opportunities and constraints. If we want to change the way we build tourism facilities in environmentally-sensitive sites, we need a new way of thinking about site planning and design, which involves a holistic approach. Sustainable site planning and design can lead to a better integration of physical facilities for tourism and their site and surroundings and can indeed help to lessen the environmental impact of these facilities.

Site planning and design for any tourism facility must clearly indicate the process of ordering human actions and works in a specific tract of land. In addition to constituting a graphic representation (to scale) that shows location, layout, general size and shape, and orientation of the different elements of the project, site planning and design should indicate the sequence of activities that make up the project, clearly establishing a space-time interaction. Also, it should ensure that all on-site human activities should have a minimum negative impact on the natural and human environment (Ceballos-Lascuráin, 2010).

Ecolodge Development around the World: The Need for True Sustainable Architecture in Ecotourism

cont'd.

The site planning and design for any ecotourism facility must be, first of all, an instrument that safeguards the sustainability and conservation of the surrounding natural and cultural heritage. Not only should it conserve the natural ecosystems but it must also contribute to repairing and restoring the environmental damages that may already be present in the site. The development of the site should strive to leave the site better off after development than before.

Zoning is a very important tool in the site planning and design process. It is the process of applying different management objectives and regulations to different parts or zones of a specific area.

The success of any tourism facility (including ecolodges, which are the appropriate facilities for ecotourism) often lies on the initial process of site evaluation and selection. Careful evaluation, in some instances, may reveal that the site is not appropriate for developing the facility. All considerations involved in selecting the most appropriate site will be essential in any forthcoming decisions dealing with design and construction.

Considering the increasing visitation to wilderness areas over the past decade and the resultant effects on the carrying capacities of the ecosystems, it would be prudent to select sites for developing ecotourism facilities that are situated just outside the nature preserves, although this is not always possible since some of the preserves are very large. As such, a well-conducted site evaluation can assist developers in finding alternatives to developing in protected areas. Selection of an appropriate site is critical for ensuring the sustainability and viability of an ecolodge.

Ecolodge Development around the World: The Need for True Sustainable Architecture in Ecotourism

cont'd.

The selected site should support the lodge within natural and biophysical resource limits while offering ecotourists the opportunity to experience and enjoy the environment (Ceballos-Lascurain, 1996).

Frequently, in those sites which are more appropriate for ecolodge development there are limited or no infrastructural elements or public services, because of typical isolation and remoteness.

It is important to analyse how much infrastructure should be provided by the local authorities, and how much by the private sector. Since the extra service demand is often only used part of the year (seasonal), and takes precedence over use by local communities, tourism providers must invest in their own infrastructure needs. Both communities and tourism sector should benefit from infrastructure development.

In every case, the private sector has an enormous responsibility in sustainable hotel planning and design, appropriate scale of development, zoning and compliance to environmental regulations. It is essential to ensure that your site plan is environmentally-friendly, minimising negative impacts on the natural landscape, local biodiversity and any existing cultural features found nearby.

Sources:

Ceballos-Lascurain, Hector. 1996. Tourism, Ecotourism and Protected Areas. IUCN. The International Unio for the Conservation of Nature. Gland, Switzerland.

Ceballos-Lascurain, Hector. 2010. Avant-propos: Le développement de l'écotourisme dans le monde. En L'Ecotourisme visité para les Acteurs Territoriaux. Presses de l'Université du Québec. Québec, Canada.

DESIGN WITH LOCAL MATERIALS

The design and style of a property should appear natural. Indeed, it should be natural in the sense that building materials are derived from the local area. In this way, buildings present an appearance harmonizing with the surrounding architectural landscapes and plant forms, complementing them instead of competing with them. After all, this natural beauty is one of the primary reasons eco-minded travelers are attracted to an area.

Design inspiration, then, may be received from a walk through the areas surrounding a site location where natural features represent the unique aspects of any particular area. Architects must ensure buildings not only complement and conform to the surroundings, but they must also be mindful of representing local design styles. Additional inspiration can and should be drawn from community members, historical and cultural contexts, and local building techniques.

Sustainable Interiors, Furnishings, and Decorating

It's a well-known saying that the best way to promote change is to be an example of change. When it comes to protecting the environment by promoting green living, one of the easiest places to start is right at home. Greening your workplace interiors, whatever your workplace may consist of, can make a big difference in reducing your global footprint.

As an added bonus, greening your interior can also lead to an immediate improvement in air quality. There are estimated to be in excess of 100,000 industrial and agricultural chemicals loose in the environment. It comes as a shock to find out that indoor air is two to five time more polluted than outside air. And with asthma on the rise, especially in children, much can be done in the area of interiors to improve air quality, and to promote sustainability.

A recent Sustainable Furnishings Council (FSC) survey reports that 30% of participants are directly affected by indoor air quality, and another 35% think everyone should care. That's a whopping

cont'd.

Sustainable Interiors, Furnishings, and Decorating

65% of prime furniture consumers. Add that to the 75% of the population who have some concerns about climate change, a number that is not affected by age or economic factors, and you have an undeniable majority of people who make sustainability a priority. 41% would buy eco friendly furnishings for themselves, 44% would buy eco friendly furnishings for their children.

And, there is quite an influence chain. As the supply of more sustainable products and furnishings increases, the percentage of the population who will make sustainable purchases will increase. And as more people become educated about the harmful effects of unsustainable consumerism, the percentage of the population that would make sustainable purchases will increase.

I love this quote from the UN Bruntland Commission in 1983, "Sustainability meets the needs of the present without compromising the needs of future generations to meet their own needs." There are several key areas to consider when it comes to sustainable interior improvements, including the effects on climate change, indoor air quality, deforestation and resource conservation, as well as the rights and wellbeing of those who manufacture the goods. It all comes back to the triple bottom line: People, Profit, Planet.

By exploring current global trends and the potential benefits of selecting environmentally safe and eco-friendly products and furnishings, I hope to encourage you to implement some of the suggestions and recommendations below.

CLIMATE CHANGE, CO2 EMISSIONS & DEFORESTATION

There has been a rise worldwide of 1.5 degrees Fahrenheit since 1900, which represents the largest increase since the end of the ice age. The estimates are for the temperatures to increase up to two degrees by 2029, an additional 5 to 7 degree increase by 2099.

Sustainable Interiors, Furnishings, and Decorating

cont'd.

This dramatic upward trend in global temperatures would bring on wholesale change for the wellbeing of future generations, as well as the wellbeing of our planet.

Research has proven that global increases in average temperatures are caused primarily by greenhouse gases, first amongst them CO_2, methane, and nitrous oxide. All of these have an anthropogenic source: human activity. 85% of CO_2 emissions are from fossil fuels: Gas, petroleum, coal and peat. The top two contributors to CO_2 emissions are, respectively, the use of energy and transportation.

Deforestation counts for the other 15%, primarily through illegal logging. Although wood is a natural, renewable resource, abusing this resource leads to dire environmental effects. If you lose a forest, you also lose a carbon sink. Therefore, losing a forest can increase CO_2 in the atmosphere simply because it is not being used up in exchange for oxygen during the process of photosynthesis. And if that forest is lost to fire, burning of wood releases greater amounts of CO_2 into the atmosphere. Deforestation is worse in the southern hemisphere, whereas Asia and especially China with its green wall of china project, have actually increased their forestation in recent years.

Water pollution is another significant concern for conservationists and sustainability experts. 97% of this planet's water is in the ocean, 2% is in the icecaps (and depleting), and only 1% makes up the ground cover, i.e. fresh water. Over half the lakes in the US are compromised, mostly due to industrial pollution. And rivers in Asia are rapidly becoming the most polluted. Textile production contributes dramatically to this pollution.

Sustainable Interiors, Furnishings, and Decorating

cont'd.

THE POSITIVE POTENTIAL OF SUSTAINABLE INTERIOR CHOICES

Home furnishings account for the third largest use of wood, after building and paper, and this is the largest industry using high quality woods. Furniture also typically makes up 4% of US landfills. Selecting sustainable alternatives when purchasing home furnishings, therefore, can have positive effects on climate change, CO_2 emissions, and deforestation. Many people think that buying green products for the home is more costly, maybe by as much as 50%. In reality, the cost difference is only 10-15% higher.

The top five ways to decrease your impact on the environment when making home furnishings design and purchase choices are:

1. Utilize legally logged and sustainably produced lumber.

2. Select fabrics and fills from more sustainable sources.

3. Use finishes with low VOC.

4. Promote local resources, products, and manufacturers (ideally within 500 miles).

5. Recycle furniture. Recycling is the mother of all resource management as it helps conserve natural resources and reduces waste. Best of all—it's one of the easiest ways and least expensive ways to redecorate! Options in the home furnishings and décor include the use of antiques, salvaged metals, and reclaimed wood. Many products these days do have recycled content. Some of the top recycling are aluminum, steel and glass. Much of the pillow stuffing available is now made of soda and water bottles (thank goodness there's a use for all those millions!). Another advantage is that it takes less energy to make products from recycled materials.

Other popular lifestyle choices include recycling at home (75% of Americans do this already), replacing traditional light bulbs with

Sustainable Interiors, Furnishings, and Decorating

cont'd. higher efficiency bulbs, adjusting the thermostat, buying green alternatives (especially cleaning supplies and paper products), replacing old or broken appliances with energy star appliances, buying more sustainable furnishings, and buying vehicles with better gas mileage.

BECOMING A SMART CONSUMER

There are several key questions to ask before making a home furnishings purchase:

Where does the wood come from that was used in this furniture or cabinetry? Where was the final piece of furniture manufactured? The closer to the wood source and ultimate purchasing point, the better. Look for furniture that was produced close to where you live and using raw materials within 500 miles. Buying local not only cuts emissions but it also supports the local community and its economy.

Was it third party certified? Look for recognized certifications such as FSC, SFI or PEFC. Of these three certifications, the FSC is the strictest with independent audits annually. Based on 56 criteria and 10 principles, and used in over 81 countries. Amongst the prime FSC criteria are prohibiting land conversion to manufacture or plantation. No unapproved pesticides. No GMO trees. Respect for the indigenous population. Annual audits. Presently, only 10% of wood used in manufacture is under FSC or any certification plan. The most certification can be found in Europe and North America, and the least in those countries with the most deforestation. Interestingly, much of this conservation effort had its beginnings under President McKinley, who in 1900 oversaw the implementation of LACY to protect habitat and wildlife. In 2008, the Lacy Act was amended to cover plants and vegetation in more detail.

Does the manufacturer have an energy use reduction plan? Remember, there is always room for improvement. With

cont'd.

Sustainable Interiors, Furnishings, and Decorating

technological advances in energy efficiency and new means of producing energy, a responsible manufacturer will have a plan in action for continued improvements.

What paints or finishes were used and are they low VOC? VOC's are harmful pollutants from certain types of varnishes, lacquers, and paints as well as many glues. Water based finishes are the best for the environment.

And finally, does the manufacturer have a socially responsible code of conduct to ensure that workers are fairly treated?

RECOMMENDATIONS FOR SUSTAINABLE HOME FURNISHINGS

There are five main points to look for in furniture to further sustainability. The frame should be made of certified wood, the panels of solid wood (not fiber board), the hardware from recycled metal, the glue from low formaldehyde, and the finishes of low VOC.

Another key factor to consider when making a purchase is the product's embodied energy. This term refers to the total energy required to turn a resource into a usable material. The total production cycle from extraction to processing, milling, all have a direct link on carbon emissions. And don't forget those vendor emissions: the energy used to transport the item and the electricity used to light the show room. Recycling saves huge energy. Aluminum, for example, requires 191 mega jewels per kilogram to make, and only 8 to recycle into something else (a 96% savings). Plastic, too, is very efficient for recycling with at 90% savings in its first reuse. Steel, 68%; and glass, 33%. Wood, because it is a natural regrowing element, is of course, very efficient. The more solid the wood products, the less embodied energy required to produce them.

Keep the following considerations in mind as you set out to make your next home furnishings purchases.

Sustainable Interiors, Furnishings, and Decorating

Wood

Plantation grown wood is one of the very best choices to ensure that the wood used in your furniture was obtained legally and responsibly. It is estimated that 15% of the hardwood used in furniture has been illegally logged, creating deforestation hotspots. To ensure that your furniture consumption does not promote this illegal activity, opt for teak, mahogany and tropical exotics grown in plantations.

Mango wood, which is a byproduct of the world's most plentiful fruit, is also very beautiful. As the trees grow fallow after 10-12 years, they must be cut and replaced.

Rubber wood is also very valuable and as a byproduct of the latex industry, they require renewal after 20+ years.

Another good choice for sustainable wood products are the rapidly renewables, which include countless grasses, bamboo (be sure it is certified as not coming from a repurposed forest), water hyacinth, rattan, cane, reed, sea grass and abaca. These are all organic materials that grow with little or no use of pesticides and can be harvested without harm within a ten-year growth cycle. That's why I chose rattan and cane as the primary materials for my two collections with LaneVenture Furniture (Chesapeake and Berkshire), and plantation grown teak and mahogany for my accessories collection with Selamat Designs.

Some notable US manufactures who are sponsoring replanting programs are Vaughan-Bassett and Guild Master.

Cushions

Cushioning in furniture is another area for improvement. Typically made of petrochemicals like Dacron, sustainable alternatives include bio foam, bio hybrids, and natural kapok wool and down.

Sustainable Interiors, Furnishings, and Decorating

Look for life cycle assessments (LCA). LCAs are the best measure of a product's effect on the environment.

Responsible Leather

Leather is problematic. While it's good because it is a byproduct of the meat industry, and while durable, highly practical, and comfortable to use, it also requires tremendous amounts of toxins to produce, especially chromium salts. The majority of leather used in the furniture industry comes from cattle raised in Brazil, transported to China or Italy for finishing, and then back to the US as a finished product for sale, the effect on the planet is large. And of course, the cows themselves are big producers of CO_2 and methane and an inefficient source of nutrition as compared to plant sources. Some options are vegetable tanning and water based dyes, using EU or US raised hides. Recently, ultra suede has made a splash and indeed it requires much less to manufacture. Actually, leather is 70% more environmentally intensive to produce than ultra suede.

Mattresses

Look for mattresses with certified wood frames, organic cotton covers, tufts holding the layers together, and the interior of pure and natural latex foam wrapped in organic wool. If springs are utilized, they should be made of recycled metal.

Window Treatments

Window treatments are important because they can also save on energy. Sustainable options include the rapid renewables such as grasses, reed and bamboos, recycled poly and organic textiles. Well-fitted window treatments, especially lined and in cold climates

---

Sustainable Interiors, Furnishings, and Decorating

---

cont'd.

with another layer of batting, can tremendously decrease energy use and are highly recommended.

Flooring

Hard surfaces are more sustainable than wall-to-wall carpet as they are long lasting and have minimal chemical finishing. They are also cheaper over the long haul as cleaning is easier. Some good choices are hardwood, ceramic tile, stained concrete, linoleum and bamboo.

Carpeting

Here is an industry that had one enormous mover for change: Lee Anderson of Anderson Carpets. Huge advances have been made since Lee started work on this and many carpets now are made with entirely recycled materials. While 5 billion pounds a year of old carpets still go into landfills, the CARE (Carpet America Recovery Effort) has done much to improve the situation. Check out their efforts at www.CarpetRecovery.org.

Over those hard services, you'll probably enjoy using some floor coverings such as natural fibers, sea grass, natural fiber wool, wool wall-to-wall, and in some bedrooms, you may prefer a traditional and tribal area rugs utilizing vegetable dyes and emphasizing traditional craftsmanship which sustains communities. Rug tying and weaving are traditional industries that have supported women and some of society's most vulnerable families for generations.

Countertops

Fortunately, natural countertops are now very in, ranging from solid stone, marble and granite, which all have lower embodied energy, to paper stone, glass and recycled glass.

cont'd.

Sustainable Interiors, Furnishings, and Decorating

Lighting

Traditional incandescent lights are inefficient, both in the initial use of energy and the additional cooling needed . A 90watt bulb is estimated to have an actual usage cost of $68 per year. Options to go with include fluorescent, LED, ceramic metal halide, and CFL. These all have much higher lumens per watt efficiency, and although some of the earlier models had much cooler colors, typically, there is only a 12-15% difference in the shade of light now and a little personal testing will soon find those that are right for your interior. An excellent way to offset a too cool but highly efficient light is to use a small 25 to 45 watt pink bulb in a side lamp that you only use when the room is in use. It's amazing how flattering a little bit of rosy lighting can be. Ditto, a pink lined lamp shade will warm up even the coolest efficient lighting.

While efficient lighting can initially be more expensive, the savings in energy typically offset the initial cost within six months. Commercial installations can see even larger savings. A 10,000 square foot store or performance space can save $10-25,000 in its first year in energy costs. The EPACT2005 tax credit is available for commercial applications.

Heating and Cooling

In most homes and lodgings, one third to one half of the electricity used is in the HVAC. A rule of thumb here is that a 1 degree Fahrenheit adjustment up or down equals a 6% energy savings. Installing ceiling fans can make a room feel 3 degrees cooler. Cleaning filters annually saves up to 10% and utilizing energy star rated appliances saves up to 40%.

Sustainable Interiors, Furnishings, and Decorating

cont'd.

We often think of awnings as decorative, but in southern climes, having awnings shade south-facing windows can result in a 60% energy savings. At night, turn the thermostat down 10 degrees from the day-time preferred temperature, and use a timed thermostat to pre-cool or pre-heat a half an hour before a space will be in use. Generally speaking, heating and cooling improvements pay for themselves in about half a year.

Water Conservation

Now that we are all watering our yard at night and during other off-peak hours and planting low-water plants and landscaping, and low flush or dual-flush toilets are becoming the norm, one of the last frontiers for water conservation is to install a low-flow shower head and to just become adjusted to taking briefer showers.

Paints and Finishes

The simplest criteria to look for when selecting paint or other coloring agent is VOC, or Volatile Organic Compounds. Be sure to select a product with low VOC. The EPA (Environmental Protection Agency) has set a limit of 350 G/L for paints. A low VOC paint might have 200 G/L. Water based finishes have a naturally low VOC, generally around 50 G/L. They dry faster and are nontoxic. VOC-free alternatives include finishes of bees wax, Tung oil, and linseed oil.

VOC emissions are prime culprits in poor indoor air quality and they are found everywhere from adhesives used in veneers, plywood, particle, and fiber board - especially highly toxic formaldehyde. VOCs are also common components of the thinners used in paint, varnishes, shellac, fabric sealers and backings, and in carpets.

Sustainable Interiors, Furnishings, and Decorating

cont'd.

GreenGuard.org performs certification on products for indoor air quality. Take a look at their website to find a list of over 10,000 chemical products. Some VOC problems can be solved by time, but out gassing does take time. An old school way to lower the VOC level in your home is to allow any new product that has a detectable odor to outgas in a garage or covered porch until the odor is no longer there. Always be sure to paint, even with low VOC, with good ventilation—keep those windows open and fans on!

Copeland Furniture has an FSC chain of custody certification, and we congratulate them on that! Purebond, from Columbia Forest Product, is a nontoxic soy-based glue. Lee has also been an industry leader, and these days, a Lee sofa will include a frame made from certified wood, springs from recycled metals, a cover of organic or natural materials, cushions of bio-hybrid foam and a fill of recycled fiber.

While making your home, lodging, or place of business more eco-friendly takes thought, time, energy and resources, the costs are well worth it and can often be almost immediately offset in savings and improved lifestyle, better air, and longer lasting, higher quality surroundings.

Sources

- Intergovernmental panel on climate change (IPCC)
- Word Meteorological Organization (WMO)
- United Nations Environmental Program (UNEP)

For free directions to hundreds of resources for green interiors: www.sustainablefurnishings.org.

Pamela Lanier is a certified Green Accredited Professional.

LOCAL BUILDING TECHNIQUES AND LABOR

After a site location and design theme have been selected, materials and local labor should be sought. In order to ensure adequate supplies and proficiently skilled laborers are available, project managers need to research and visit the appropriate venues sourcing such resources.

After an initial assessment, recognize any indigenous limitations and alter plans accordingly. Some regions may present a scarcity of building materials, in which case the potential for repurposed materials or structures (such as shipment containers, repurposed airplanes, or recycled wood) may be an appropriate solution. Conversely, some regions may offer an abundance of previously unacknowledged resources, or more affordable ones (such as cob or rammed earth). Thorough research and planning will allow you to make appropriate region-specific decisions on building techniques and materials.

The importance of sourcing local labor cannot be overstated. This commitment brings income to the community, builds rapport between a new establishment and its neighbors, and provides relevant knowledge and techniques that are convenient and address avoidable dilemmas. Such conveniences include pest control and temperature regulation, considerations that ought to be intrinsic to building design and technique. Knowledge of the appropriate and best building methods vary by region and are possibly even more unique in particular locales.

Offsetting Travel Emissions

Dan Linsky

Let's go! One of the most enthusiastic phrases we can ever exclaim. We're going on vacation, or on a prosperous business trip, or any number of other reasons why we leave the comfort of our homes and drive, fly, sail, or rail. And all of us, or many of us, ok at least some of us, want to travel in such a way as to have the least negative impact on the environment. One of the environmental impacts of travel is emitting greenhouse gas.

In most cases we do not have the ability, or funds, to install technology that would reduce the emissions of the plane, car, train, or ship that we are travelling on. However, we can calculate the amount of GHG emissions that result from our travel, and pay to reduce an equal amount of emissions on projects that have been undertaken solely for that purpose. Since climate change, caused by the emission of greenhouse gases by human activities, is a global pollution, emissions that take place anywhere in the world have the same negative impact. Conversely, emission reductions can take place anywhere (in your vehicle, or on a project somewhere in the world) and have the same positive impact in the fight against climate change.

That greenhouse gas emission reduction is commonly referred to as a carbon offset. Simply put, a carbon offset is a reduction in emissions of carbon dioxide or other greenhouse gases made in order to compensate for (or to offset) an emission made elsewhere. One carbon offset equals one metric tonne of CO_2 equivalent reduced.

cont'd

Offsetting Travel Emissions

So what should you look for when offsetting your travel emissions by purchasing offsets? First, find a carbon calculator that you trust. Trustworthy calculators should include, or link to, an explanation behind their calculations, and use regularly recognized data and emission factors. A web search for "carbon calculator" will bring up many calculator choices. It is recommended that you find one that is easy to use, and offers a simple calculation for what you want to offset, in this case travel, as opposed to one that requires you to calculate the emissions resulting from all aspects of your life (unless of course you want to offset all of your carbon emissions). The more complex calculators are time consuming, especially if you just want to offset your travel emissions. Finding a calculator, and actually calculating the emissions resulting from your travel is the easy part. Finding quality carbon offsets can be a bit tougher.

Be careful to only buy quality offsets, based on four standards: additionality, prevention of leakage, permanence and verifiability.

Additionality:

Additionality means that a project is beyond business as usual. In other words, the GHG reductions wouldn't have happened if the project site went about its normal business, or is regulated regarding carbon emissions, or would not have been possible without the revenue gained from selling offsets. The point is to ensure that any greenhouse gas reductions from the project are 'in addition' to what would have happened anyway.

Otherwise offsets from the project don't achieve any extra environmental good.

Offsetting Travel Emissions

Prevention of Leakage:

Leakage typically occurs in situations where resources are being protected. For example, if a carbon offset program focuses on protecting a forest from being logged, it's entirely possible that loggers might just move their operations down the road to another forest. In this case, the emissions weren't really reduced, they just took place at a different site.

Permanence:

Permanence is typically a concern with forestry projects or other projects where greenhouse gases are being stored, rather than reduced or destroyed. If there is significant risk that the stored carbon would be released through events such as a forest fire or a leak from sequestered carbon, the project developer should make evident the steps they've taken to avoid leakage, and perhaps even offer to supply other types of offsets to the buyer in the case the stored carbon is released.

Verifiability:

The last requirement is verifiability. An objective, qualified, third party, other than the project developer, must be able to look at project data and confirm that the carbon reductions are real and credible. The third-party verifier determines proper baselines and verifies that the reductions adhere to strict monitoring and reporting standards.

It is very difficult for most individuals to test for the criteria above. Here's the short cut. Purchase offsets from projects that are registered at a credible carbon offset registry. Examples of these include the Climate Action Reserve, American Carbon Registry, and the Verified Carbon Standard among others.

	Offsetting Travel Emissions
cont'd	All of these registries require projects to meet the above criteria.

There are additional criteria you may look for that don't affect the quality of the offsets, but might be important to you, the buyer. For example, one personal criterion may include the location of the offset project, although location doesn't matter as far as climate change is concerned, some people have a heart for certain areas, whether it's close to home, a developing country, etc.

Ultimately, if we expect big corporations to be environmentally conscious, we must expect the same from ourselves. Offsetting your travel emissions to make your trip carbon neutral is simple and inexpensive. Most importantly, you really are helping reduce greenhouse gas emissions, as these projects would not take place without the purchase of the offsets they create, and doing your part in the fight against climate change. And for that I thank you.

Dan Linsky, ClimeCo

Note: See Resources for more on carbon offsets.

CONCORDIA ECO RESORT

St. John, US Virgin Islands, USA

www.concordiaeco-resort.com

The primary economic activity in the United States Virgin Islands is tourism. The balmy island weather, white sand beaches, and pristine coral reefs offer a tropical paradise for avid divers, snorkelers, island hoppers, honeymooners, and nature lovers alike. Amidst the all-inclusive resorts and skyscraping hotels, Concordia Eco-Resort stands out as an example of successful ecotourism.

Built in 1976, Concordia Eco Resort was established before the term ecotourism had yet gained momentum. Founder and architect, Stanley Selengut, had a vision of a vacation destination that offered an affordable, sustainable means for nature enthusiasts to spend their holiday enveloped in the wild and surrounded by likeminded individuals with access to basic comforts. Concordia Eco Resort embodies the philosophy that "environmental sensitivity, human comfort and responsible consumption are all compatible and can also enhance your vacation experience."

Pain-staking considerations were given to site location, construction methods, material use, and energy efficiency in the establishment of Concordia. The resort was designed as a pedestrian community. As such, elevated walkways were built in place of paved pathways, leaving the ground foliage below untouched and allowing plants and wildlife to continue on their way undisturbed. Favoring walking as a means of transportation over any motorized vehicle prevented soil erosion that would have resulted from the construction of roads, which would have washed topsoil into the ocean, smothering the coral along the coast on which the marine life depends. The tent cottages were built by hand in order to avoid destructive construction activity, and used recycled building materials wherever possible, such as "plastic lumber", recycled glass tiles and tire rugs. Much of the facility is powered by the sun through high-efficiency photovoltaic roof panels that use that provide energy for lights, appliances and other equipment.

In a place with no lakes, aquifers or permanent surface water supply, Concordia has optimized its use of fresh water. Rain water catchments installed on almost every building collect about 345,000 gallons of rainwater each year, enough to supply the laundry, housekeeping facilities and the bathhouses. Even wastewater is turned into a usable resource. Each day, between 2,000 and 7,000 gallons of wastewater are produced. The resort treats this water through a system (designed by Santec Corporation) that uses nature's own bacteria and gravity to produce a clear liquid rich in nutrients ready to be transported through lateral water lines to an adjacent terraced organic orchard where bananas, oranges, okra, limes, lemons, luffa gourds and papaya are grown. A combination of low-flush toilets, waterless urinals (made by The Waterless Company), and odorless composting toilets (we recommend www.compostingtoilet.org) minimize water use and impact on the environment and maximize conservation.

Concordia has placed equal weight on processing its waste. Each guest is briefed on the facility's recycling program and encouraged to participate by sorting their trash into the appropriate recycling bins. Blue bins are located throughout the camp and 100% of all aluminum cans, glass, and clear plastic bottles are recycled. In a creative twist on the common saying, "one man's trash is another man's treasure," Concordia instated a Trash to Treasure Program that remanufactures waste glass bottles, aluminum cans, waste paper and used linens into marketable objects and souvenir gifts to sell in gift shop. These items include glass blown floor tiles, paper weights, and elaborate glass objects made out of recycled glass bottles, as well as coat hooks, door pulls and coasters made out of melted aluminum cans.

Attention to detail has yielded a spotless ecotourism reputation for this longtime resort. In every step and at every level, Concordia Eco Resort has supported ecotourism. In its wake, the local flora and fauna remain intact, nearby coastlines experience minimum impacts, and tourists leave with a greater appreciation and understanding of St. John's native wildlife.

BARDESSONO

Yountville, California, USA

www.bardessono.com

Image courtesy of Bardessono.

Bardessono exquisitely demonstrates how an upscale lodging establishment can uphold environmental values while offering a luxurious guest experience. The hotel has been designed to achieve the Leadership in Energy and Environmental Design's (LEED) Platinum certification, the highest standard for environmental design, and features the following:

■ Minimal offsite energy use, enabled by the 200-kilowatt solar energy system (high efficiency solar panels cover the roofs) that provides approximately one-half the total electrical energy requirement of the property.

■ All buildings designed to reduce heat gain from summer sun but allow winter sun to warm rooms.

■ All window glass is reduced temperature transfer "Low-E."

■ 72,300-foot well on property is paired with a ground source heat pump to utilize ground water (which remains stable throughout the year at about 70 degrees Fahrenheit) to moderate in-room temperature.

Salvaged wood, repurposed and recycled materials used in construction and design elements.

■ All glues, adhesives, finishes, paints, carpets and fabrics used at Bardessono meet VOC standards (Low Volatile Organic Compounds).

The creek is buffered by a minimum of 35 feet of native riparian plants rather than development in order to create a healthy vegetative environment for native animals and fish, as well as minimize any silting of the creek through runoff.

These environmental initiatives minimize the impacts of construction and design and integrate the most advanced environmental technologies.

MAXIMIZING SELF-EFFICIENCY

Building and operating an ecotourism establishment requires significant amounts of energy, making it critical to take advantage of technological advances in energy efficiency. While in the planning phases, project managers should ascertain the viability of solar, wind, geothermal, and hydroelectric energy options in the area.

Onsite food production—Slow food/farm-to-table

Benefits of

- ■ Employ local Ag techniques
- ■ Use your own compost
- ■ Irrigation options
- ■ Introduce tourists to local cuisine

The Basics of Ethnobotany

By Kathleen Harrison

Ethnobotany: What is it?

Ethnobotany is the study of the relationship between plants and humans. Ethno signifies people, culture; botany is the study of plant life.

Why is it interesting?

Our lives depend on plants. All cultures around the world have always relied on plants for food, medicine, clothing, fuel, and the structures we live in. Plants provide the materials for containers, ropes, tools, weapons, and musical instruments. The plant world is woven into all our mythology, our rituals, and our artwork. The beauty of nature surrounds us— we are rooted in plants. Even modern manufacturing uses numerous plant oils, fibers, and chemicals from plants. Forests breathe in CO_2, which keeps the planet cool enough. By exhaling oxygen, plants refresh our atmosphere, so that we can breathe. The old knowledge of what grew in the forests, meadows, coastlines, and even deserts expressed itself in ways of tending nature. It seems that the time has come for us to remember or dream up new and old ways of tending nature, for the good of all species.

How might ethnobotany promote conservation?

Traditionally, people cared for the health of nature and their immediate environment because it fed them, clothed them, healed them. We were handed down instructions on the ongoing care of the land and waters. All of our ancestors were raised on the old stories, myths and rituals that illustrate the cycles of nature.

The Basics of Ethnobotany

cont'd

Every culture had ways of passing on the instructions for how to be stewards of our sustainable environment and how to respect all the beings in it. All this is ethnobotany, ethnobiology. Conservation might be promoted by cultivating a renewed awareness of these relations and practices, such as:

- How to tend a forest, using some trees and leaving others to increase the health of the forest.
- How to harvest ocean species of fish and seaweeds, so that they will become more abundant rather than depleted.
- How to respect the rivers, where they might flow, and not try to force their channels to meet our needs.
- How to keep some hardy types of grains, fruits and vegetables going, to plant in the drought years, or in the flood years.
- How to pass on that knowledge of appropriate relationship to nature's resources and moods.
- The study of ethnobotany also increases respect for the cultures that have not forgotten all their old ways. Cultural diversity is linked to biodiversity; a mountain-culture's language includes the names and instructions on how to conserve that mountain's resources. The stories that go with planting time, harvest time, hunting time are the illustrations of that culture's relationship with its homeland. Eco means home. Ecology is the study of home.
- What are good places to visit to learn or observe ethnobotany?

The indigenous people of any area on earth know an incredible amount about which plants are useful, which are healing, which are poisonous, and stories about how they got that way. A visit to Native Americans in the U.S. or Canada can show how people of that place use and care for their plant life. Once you are looking for examples of ethnobotany in action, the inquisitive traveler finds innumerable examples among the native people of Central America, South America, Southeast Asia, Indonesia, India, China (all of Asia, of course),

The Basics of Ethnobotany

cont'd

Africa, and even the Mediterranean and Europe. Around the world, people have depended on plants for their livelihood from the beginning of humanity, so the evidence is everywhere.

Examples:

Bali, Indonesia –

Threads of Life supports traditional Indonesian textile arts and artists. English-speaking experts provide educational lectures and lead tours of Indonesian textile making, weaving and dyeing with local, natural fibers and dyes.

www.threadsoflife.com

Threads of Life recommends many other travel and cultural art organizations in Asia that use appropriate technology while preserving traditional culture. Links are here:

http://www.threadsoflife.com/links.asp#travel

Oaxaca, Mexico –

This region of southern Mexico is full of fascinating examples of living ethnobotany. Oaxaca is the name of both the large, mountainous state and its capital, a lovely city with a colonial center. The city is surrounded by villages that each specialize in a particular craft or art form, and by ruins of previous societies, the ancestors of current Oaxacans. It is a region respected for its surviving cultural diversity, with many indigenous languages still being spoken. The region is best known for its amazing textiles, mostly woven rugs made from wool and dyed with local plants and minerals. Many weavers' homes are open to public visits, so you can see them at work and buy directly from the weavers. The region is also renowned for its excellent and distinctive cuisine, with varieties of foods and flavors that are grown nearby.

Carvings, ceramics, costumes and fiestas are all part of local culture. The Museum of Textiles is a remarkable display of the fibers and dyes they use.

The Basics of Ethnobotany

cont'd

The Santo Domingo Ethnobotanical Garden is a treasure for both education and beauty. Oaxaca is one of this author's favorite places in the world.

Hawaii, the Big Island –

Yes, there is culture in Hawaii beyond the tourist trail. Native Polynesians came in waves over the past 1500 years, evolving their traditions as they populated the islands. The Big Island of Hawaii has hidden treasures if you know where to go. Ruins, ethnobotanical gardens, native Hawaiian practitioners who show their deep knowledge of nature in song, healing, hula, herbal medicine, ceremony, and the crafting of tools, textiles, utensils, musical instruments, and storytelling — all including plant life!

A great way to learn this approach to the Polynesian/Hawaiian worldview (and to have a lot of fun) is to take an intensive travel course with an expert ethnobotanist and a Hawaiian cultural practitioner: Kathleen Harrison and Momi Subiono gather and guide a small group of people through the ethnobotany of Hawaii in their annual course, Little Planet, Big Island. Learn to understand this way of relating to plants, make herbal medicine, eat great organic local food, and visit the beach, the forest, and the live volcano. For more information about upcoming courses, contact kat@botanicaldimensions.org

What is Aquaponic Gardening and Why Might You Care?

By Sylvia Bernstein

What if I told you that you could catch fish for dinner right in your own backyard? And what if before you catch those fish they were growing the veggies for the rest of your dinner plate? Would you believe me? You should! This is all within reach using a new style of gardening called Aquaponics.

Aquaponics is, at its most basic level, the marriage of aquaculture (raising fish) and hydroponics (growing plants in water and without soil) together in one integrated system. The fish waste provides organic food for the growing plants and the plants naturally filter the water in which the fish live. The third and fourth critical, yet invisible actors in the play are the beneficial bacteria and composting red worms. Think of them as the Conversion Team. The beneficial bacteria exist on every moist surface of an aquaponic system. They convert the ammonia from the fish waste that is toxic to the fish and useless to the plants, first into nitrites and then into nitrates. The nitrates are relatively harmless to the fish and most importantly, they make terrific plant food. At the same time, the worms convert the solid waste and decaying plant matter in your aquaponic system into vermicompost.

Here is the rest of the story

- Aquaponic Gardening enables home fish farming. You can now feel good about eating fish again.
- Aquaponic Gardening uses 90% less water than soil-based gardening because the water is recirculated and only that which the plants take up or evaporates is ever replaced.
- Aquaponic Gardening results in two crops for one input (fish feed).

What is Aquaponic Gardening and Why Might You Care?

cont'd

- Aquaponic Gardening is four to six times as productive on a square foot basis as soil-based gardening. This is because with aquaponic gardening, you can pack plants about twice as densely as you can in soil and the plants grow two to three times as fast as they do in soil.

- Aquaponic systems only require a small amount of energy to run a pump and aeration for the fish. This energy can be provided through renewable methods.

- Aquaponics does not rely on the availability of good soil, so it can be set-up anywhere, including inner city parking lots, abandoned warehouses, schools, restaurants, home basements and garages.

- Aquaponic Gardening is free from weeds, watering and fertilizing concerns, and because it is done at a waist-high level, there is no back strain.

- Aquaponic Gardening is necessarily organic. Natural fish waste provides all the food the plants need. Pesticides would be harmful to the fish so they are never used. Hormones, antibiotics, and other fish additives would be harmful to the plants so they are never used. And the result is every bit as flavorful as soil-based organic produce, with the added benefit of fresh fish for a safe, healthy source of protein.

- Aquaponics is completely scalable. The same basic principles apply to a system based on a 10 gallon aquarium as to a commercial operation.

- Aquaponic gardens are straight forward to set up and operate in your own backyard or home as long as you follow some basic guidelines. They can even be constructed using recycled materials, including liquid shipping containers and old bathtubs. Or purchase a system kit if you are not very DIY-inclined. The main point is to set a system soon and become fish independent! There is simply no reason to rely on the fish counter anymore.

What is Aquaponic Gardening and Why Might You Care?

cont'd

- Efficient waste management
- Reduce, reuse, recycle
- Composting toilets
- Water efficiency, grey water collection and uses
- Gravity-fed
- Additionally, the natural slopes of a site location may present the option of gravity-fed water supplies and ought to be considered as this delivery eliminates pumps and expensive electric requirements to move water.

Sylvia Bernstein is president of The Aquaponic Source and author of "Aquaponic Gardening."

INN SERENDIPITY

Browntown, Wisconsin, USA

www.innserendipity

Photo courtesy of John D. Ivanko/farmsteadchef.com

Inn Serendipity innkeepers have perfected the art of balance between personal and professional life by blending the two inextricably. This husband and wife innkeeping duo have incorporated their personal beliefs of environmental sustainability, equity and social justice into their every-day business model. The result is a bed and breakfast that offers comfortable stays and allows guests to experience the bounties of nature first-hand.

At its core, this sustainable business model involves striving for self-sufficiency. The inn is entirely powered by renewable energy, including a 10 kW wind turbine and a .7 kW photovoltaic system. The inn also boasts an all-electric CitiCar, which is recharged by a .5 kW off-grid photovoltaic system on site. All meals are prepared mostly from the organic fruits, vegetables and herbs grown on-site in the organic garden and solar-heated straw-bale greenhouse. All of these efforts, in addition to participating in various carbon offset programs, result in the inn operating as a carbon-negative business, meaning that more carbon dioxide is sequestered annually than is emitted from business operations and lifestyle.

Through years of operation and constant efforts to improve sustainability and conservation efforts, Inn Serendipity has become a star example of maximizing self-sufficiency.

CAMP DENALI

Denali National Park, Alaska, USA

www.campdenali.com

Photo courtesy of Camp Denali

Alaska in its entirety is a call to the wild. Back in 1954, founders of Camp Denali answered this call by establishing one of the first wilderness lodges in Alaska. Surrounded by nearly six million acres of Denali National Park and Preserve, Camp Denali offers guests a simple, close-to-nature vacation experience that provides educational opportunities to learn about the Alaskan wilderness and local ecology.

The original lodge and guest cabins are 90 miles from the nearest power grid. This characteristic encouraged the use and development of renewable energy sources such as hydroelectricity from the free-flowing spring water on an adjacent mountainside, solar electricity from photovoltaic panels, and solar-heated water for use in the kitchen, bathrooms and dining hall. As an additional means to reduce energy consumption, staff line-dry most of their laundry on outdoor clotheslines.

A remote location also has implications when it comes to food. To help put a dent in the lodge's dependence on outside food, a large greenhouse was built onsite and a number of outdoor raised herb and vegetable beds provide organic, seasonal produce. This farm-to-table practice of growing part of their own produce supports the lodge's mission to live close to the land.

Camp Denali is mindful of its ecological footprint in a number of additional ways. To minimize the impact on the land and wildlife, the numerous hiking destinations are rotated throughout the summer. Most importantly, a practice of "Leave No Trace" is practiced by all staff and heavily encouraged for all guests when exploring the Denali wilderness.

Camp Denali exemplifies ecotourism at its rawest. It offers basic accommodation for ecotourists to use as launch pads to explore the Denali wilderness and to learn about its ecology and history. Over the past sixty years, it has remained true to its original philosophy and calling to "stay small, maintain a minimal footprint on the land, and provide comfortable hospitality that allows visitors to experience the wild nature of Denali National Park."

3

Community Development

TOURISM CAN BE A KEY DRIVER FOR LOCAL COMMUNITY
development. When proper planning and design of a tourism operation
are in place, the positive economic returns can be used to maintain and
improve the host community's standard of living and quality of life. This
can be achieved through a number of initiatives, including improvements to
infrastructure and telecommunications, education, training, and healthcare.
Not to mention, tourism in protected areas can also ensure sustainable
growth in the host community by emphasizing the value of local arts and
culture as well as the importance of native environmental sites and wildlife,
all of which contribute to the initial motivators that generate tourism to the
area in the first place. As one of its central pillars, ecotourism aims to support
and strengthen the local community.

A successful tourism destination must be accessible. Therefore, tourism
operators must invest in the infrastructure and telecommunication of
the local and surrounding communities. This includes maintaining and
upgrading roads, promoting sustainable means of transportation to and from
the protected area, and building communications networks such as landline
telephones, cellular phone towers, internet access, etc. The importance lies in
physically and remotely connecting tourists and the greater outside world to
the local villages and protected area.

Additionally, ecotourism businesses often partner with existing non-profit organizations or create new organizations whose purpose is to raise funds to support local community projects. This includes projects to increase access to clean water, improve agricultural practices and access to farmable lands, build community centers, or collect donations from tourists and the outside world to provide basic materials and supplies to local schools, children, and families in need. Providing these services and resources is a direct way that tourism can have a beneficial impact on community development.

Ecotourism facilities promote local hiring in order to increase local income and employment. Oftentimes, the employer provides all employees with basic language, literacy and numeracy training, which increases the educational level of the local community. These are transferable skills which can then be applied in the greater community. In a similar spirit, tourism businesses can also be a place for training in other skills such as agricultural practices, power generating technologies, food hygiene, mechanical proficiency, and much more. These are practical skills that can be shared and spread throughout the community.

Some of the most popular tourism destinations include protected areas, which offer nearly untouched sceneries and wildlife and are often isolated. These remote areas too often do not have sufficient medical and healthcare facilities. These basic needs often accompany the development of tourism because tourists demand a safe vacation environment. Therefore, tourism can be the vehicle used to bring basic healthcare to remote protected areas.

A looming threat that the introduction of tourism poses to host communities is the dilution of local values and cultures through the introduction to foreign cultures. This threat can be mitigated by encouraging the preservation of native culture, crafts and the arts. This can be achieved by ensuring the continued availability of supplies used in local arts and crafts, memorializing and documenting cultural traditions, and perhaps facilitating cultural education. When an ecotourism facility properly educates and informs its visitors about local values and culture and provides appropriate and noninvasive ways for visitors to interact with local inhabitants, it improves intercultural understanding and helps ensure that the native cultural identity remains intact for generations to come.

Ecotourism also has the capability to educate the public, both visitors and locals, about native environmental sites and wildlife. Education about the value of the native habitat is the first step in encouraging and supporting local conservation efforts and raising funds to protect sites of significance. This may lead to the discovery of new ways to utilize a native resource to create sustainable products, such as artwork made of local materials, sustainable fishing, or supporting a service-based industry.

There are a number of ways to measure the positive impacts of tourism on community development. The infrastructure and telecommunications impacts can be measured in increased access to recreation sites, protected areas, or subsistence resources, while the impacts of education and training can be measured in increased school graduation rates and a decrease in unemployment. Health and medical developments lead to reduced infant mortality and increased availability of basic healthcare to treat both minor and major health problems. Environmental education can lead to improved water and air quality, an increase in native wildlife, and a decrease in harmful or unsustainable living practices (such as overfishing, overhunting, over-farming, etc.).

By maximizing the amount of money that remains in the local community through the use of locally-owned accommodations, the employment of local people, and the support of local services, including agricultural products and arts, ecotourism can fund local community projects and initiatives that support community development. Ecotourism helps preserve and raise awareness of delicate and protected areas, promotes the development of cultural pride and confidence in the local community, invests in sustainable development through construction projects and social education, and contributes a net positive effect on its surroundings.

Sustainable Tourism and Fair Trade

By Candi Horton

An Overview

The sale of fair trade products as one component in sustainable tourism can enhance your customers' experience and strengthen your business.

Sustainable Tourism and Fair Trade

cont'd

The sale of fair trade products as one component in sustainable tourism can enhance your customers' experience and strengthen your business.

When offering fair trade gifts to your clientele, you:

- Create local jobs
- Provide additional revenue for your business
- Educate your customers about fair trade and your culture
- Give your customers a physical remembrance of their experience with you that can promote discussion in their home community and encourage others to consider sustainable tourism and shopping fair trade

Fair trade products are made by marginalized artisans without a ready market for their goods in their own communities. The sale of fair trade goods provides jobs while encouraging ecological sustainability, capacity building, and cultural awareness.

Members of the Fair Trade Federation in North America uphold these nine fair trade principles:

1. *Create Opportunities for Economically and Socially Marginalized Producers*—Fair Trade is a strategy for poverty alleviation and sustainable development. Members create social and economic opportunities through trading partnerships with marginalized producers. Members place the interests of producers and their communities as the primary concern of their enterprises.

2. *Develop Transparent and Accountable Relationships*—Fair Trade involves relationships that are open, fair, consistent, and respectful. Members show consideration for both customers and producers by sharing information about the entire trading chain through honest and proactive communication.

Sustainable Tourism and Fair Trade

cont'd

They create mechanisms to help customers and producers feel actively involved in the trading chain. If problems arise, members work cooperatively with fair trade partners and other organizations to implement solutions.

3. *Build Capacity*—Fair Trade is a means to develop producers' independence. Members maintain long-term relationships based on solidarity, trust, and mutual respect, so that producers can improve their skills and their access to markets. Members help producers to build capacity through proactive communication, financial and technical assistance, market information, and dialogue. They seek to share lessons learned, to spread best practices, and to strengthen the connections between communities, including among producer groups.

4. *Promote Fair Trade*—Fair Trade encourages an understanding by all participants of their role in world trade. Members actively raise awareness about Fair Trade and the possibility of greater justice in the global economic system. They encourage customers and producers to ask questions about conventional and alternative supply chains and to make informed choices. Members demonstrate that trade can be a positive force for improving living standards, health, education, the distribution of power, and the environment in the communities with which they work.

5. *Pay Promptly and Fairly*—Fair Trade empowers producers to set prices within the framework of the true costs of labor time, materials, sustainable growth, and related factors. Members take steps to ensure that producers have the capacity to manage this process. Members comply with or exceed international, national, local, and, where applicable, Fair Trade Minimum standards for their employees and producers.

Sustainable Tourism and Fair Trade

cont'd

Members seek to ensure that income is distributed equitably at all times, particularly equal pay for equal work by women and men. Members ensure prompt payment to all of their partners. Producers are offered access to interest-free pre-harvest or pre-production advance payment.

6. *Support Safe and Empowering Working Conditions*—Fair Trade means a safe and healthy working environment free of forced labor. Throughout the trading chain, members cultivate workplaces that empower people to participate in the decisions that affect them. Members seek to eliminate discrimination based on race, caste, national origin, religion, disability, gender, sexual orientation, union membership, political affiliation, age, marital, or health status. Members support workplaces free from physical, sexual, psychological, or verbal harassment or abuse.

7. *Ensure the Rights of Children*—Fair Trade means that all children have the right to security, education, and play. Throughout the trading chain, Members respect and support the UN Convention on the Rights of the Child, as well as local laws and social norms. Members disclose the involvement of children in production. Members do not support child trafficking and exploitative child labor.

8. *Cultivate Environmental Stewardship*—Fair Trade seeks to offer current generations the ability to meet their needs without compromising the ability of future generations to meet their own needs. Members actively consider the implications of their decisions on the environment and promote the responsible stewardship of resources. Members reduce, reuse, reclaim, and recycle materials wherever possible. They encourage environmentally sustainable practices throughout the entire trading chain.

Sustainable Tourism and Fair Trade

cont'd

9. *Respect Cultural Identity*—Fair Trade celebrates the cultural diversity of communities, while seeking to create positive and equitable change. Members respect the development of products, practices, and organizational models based on indigenous traditions and techniques to sustain cultures and revitalize traditions. Members balance market needs with producers' cultural heritage.

Product —The specifics

Consider working with your local artisan groups to create products from the following list. Each product should include a cultural, experiential, or local material component.

Christmas ornaments

Ornaments should be designed to be lightweight in order to hang easily and when possible two-sided. They should be made of a local material or denote a cultural motif or include the name of the country, region, or site.

Bracelets, pins, and earrings

These are easy to pack and may be purchased in multiples for those taking home gifts to family and friends.

Coin purses

Use traditional designs and materials with modern hardware. Make sure zippers are of good quality or use Velcro closures. Make sure the sizing easily fits credit cards along with coins. Consider sizing for cell phones.

Tote bags

These could be from local recycled materials or locally made fabrics or materials. Your guests have likely packed light. They may need to purchase an additional carry-on bag or a sturdier and larger check-through bag.

Sustainable Tourism and Fair Trade

cont'd

Scarves

If your community has a traditional textile heritage or technique, scarves are a perfect product. While the regional techniques will be appreciated, some attention will need to be given to color combinations. A few purists will want colors that are regionally appropriate and historically accurate. You should have some of these. You will sell more of the colors that are currently in fashion in North America. These are generally not the same.

Headbands and hats

Headbands can again utilize local textiles and make great gifts to take home. Hats styled to be of the most use while they are on their visit can sell well.

Cards

Should you have a paper-making heritage in your region, put that to use here. Where there is no paper-making tradition, cards will still sell well using cultural motifs or local pictures or photos.

Toys and games

If there is a local toy or game make it available for your visitor to take home. Include instructions.

Details that increase sales

Packaging and shipping

Be ready to package purchases in a way that will make your customer feel at ease with transporting them home. Costs incurred to do this should be incorporated into your retail price.

Sustainable Tourism and Fair Trade

cont'd

Should you have larger items that are not easily transported by hand, look into shipping options and provide this service for your clientele. Many are happy to pay the additional cost to have a one-of-a-kind piece grace their home.

Include hang tags or information sheets for each product

Include information on the product. How does it help the artisan? What is it made of? What is its cultural or historical significance? This information can be attached to the product or be included in the product display for them to pick up as needed.

Signed by the artisan

Making a personal connection with the person who made the product adds value for the purchaser and increases sales. A photo of the artisan at work as part of the product display also helps highlight the product.

An educated staff

Everyone involved in selling fair trade products should be trained in sales techniques and educated about each product, material, and technique.

Price ranges

Include a range of prices in your selection. You will need some items that can be purchased in bulk at lower price ranges for gift-giving to friends and family. Higher end items should not be neglected, visitors are willing to spend on themselves when there is perceived cultural value. You must have other items in each price category however in order to sell the higher end pieces, there should not be a pricing gap. These steps in pricing help sell higher end items.

cont'd

Sustainable Tourism and Fair Trade

Conclusion

As you establish the sale of fair trade products you will want to keep detailed records of which pieces sell. Generally, eighty percent of your sales will come from twenty percent of your products. Those top selling products should be well stocked at all times and quantities on hand always monitored to ensure a "never out" status.

The slower selling pieces will need to be phased out to make room for new items that may become your bestsellers.

Candi Horton, Baksheesh Fair Trade, Sonoma and St. Helena, California

ECOVENTURA

The Galapagos, Ecuador

www.ecoventura.com

Photo courtesy of Ecoventura.

Ecoventura is a family-owned, ecologically-conscious cruise company that shares the beauty and bounty of the Galapagos with a limited number of ecotourists each year. Ecoventura's fleet comprises of four 20-passenger motor yachts and employs a small guide-to-passenger ratio (one expert guide for every ten passengers). During the seven or fourteen day tours offered by Ecoventura, all tourists soak in the beauties of the islands, but always in the company of an expert naturalist guide to reduce potential environmental impacts and wildlife harassment.

Ecoventura is a proven leader in community development. This cruise company is involved in a wide array of projects and organizations dedicated to supporting the population of San Cristobal Island through employment opportunities, purchasing local products and sponsorship of a local school and non-profit. Ecoventura is a supporter of "Gotitas de Esperanza" (Drops of Hope), a foundation that sponsors the salaries of teachers and physical therapists at a local school who work with children with Down's Syndrome and other physical disabilities and adults who are hearing impaired. Guests aboard the Ecoventura cruises are encouraged to participate in a project called "Pack for a Purpose," in which guests pack five pounds of donation items needed by local children. In 2006, Ecoventura established the Galapagos Marine Biodiversity Fund in partnership with the World Wildlife Fund that supports environmental education and marine conservation by strengthening the local communities' ability to manage natural resources. Most recently in 2012, Ecoventura partnered with The Ecology Project to develop a career-shadowing program that provides high school students with an opportunity to explore a career as a naturalist guide while aboard one of the yachts for a one-week session with existing guides serving as mentors.

Whether it be in the Galapagos or around the world, other tour organizations can learn much from this leader in sustainability.

GULUDO BEACH LODGE

Guludo, Kenya

www.guludo.com

Photo courtesy of Guludo Beach Lodge.

For a successful and sustainable example of a business that has established an organization to support its community projects, look no further than

Guludo Beach Lodge. The owners of this lodging establishment are also the founders of the Nema Foundation, a charity that partners with sixteen local communities to implement projects that tackle the root causes of poverty and environmental devastation.

The lodge operates based on fair trade practices and minimizing environmental impact. This includes promoting local employment and locally purchasing goods and services that minimize packaging and are sourced from renewable and sustainable sources. As ongoing goals, the lodge makes every effort to reduce pollution, emissions, non-renewable energy use, minimize and manage waste responsibly, use water and energy efficiently, and minimize the use of harmful chemicals and toxic products. Guludo Beach Lodge is also involved in protecting and conserving the natural environment and wildlife in and around the lodge.

The lodge supports the charity by donating 5% of all revenue to Nema. These funds are used to support ongoing projects such as a water point rehabilitation project that provides access to clean water for 20,000 people, provides daily school meals to 800 malnourished children, offers a secondary school scholarship for 129 scholars, has constructed two primary schools, and so much more. Nema is also actively involved in providing household training in nutrition, malaria, HIV, hygiene, and sanitation to the local community. Nema invests in the future of the local community.

Guludo Beach Lodge and Nema are a wonderful example of how to achieve a profitable business while supporting the environment as well as the local community.

4

Environmental
Stewardship

ENVIRONMENTAL STEWARDSHIP INCLUDES ALL EFFORTS TO SUPPORT environmental sustainability projects. An ecotourism operation might create a new conservation organization or simply support an existing local group. Environmental stewardship also includes offering community, guest, and staff trainings and seminars that promote environmental education. The important takeaway is that an ecotourism operation needs to be proactive in conserving, preserving, and protecting the native natural surroundings.

There are countless ways for an ecotourism business to support environmental protection efforts. One popular example is initiating a volunteer program that provides guests and visitors with an opportunity to participate in hands-on projects such as planting native plants and trees, cleaning a local beach or coastline, or supporting native wildlife by conserving the native habitats. Other options include donating a share of annual profits to a well-known, respected nature organization or collecting guest donations to support a local conservation project. Supporting local biodiversity and natural heritage are important components of ecotourism.

A wonderful way to boost your business's sustainability credibility, and not to mention attracting the right kind of conscious traveler, is to invest in education. Being a useful and relevant source for good green travel practices will help build a healthy reputation. Ways to promote environmental education include offering trainings, classes, seminars, or any combination of the three to the local community, traveling guests, and staff that emphasize the benefits of responsible travel and the value of native natural resources. Contributing to a higher global understanding of sustainability practices will encourage tourists around the world to adapt their travel practices and seek out alternative ways to travel, a big win for ecotourism all over the planet.

WWOOF: Sustainable Travel Meets Sustainable Food

By Patricia Apple

Today's current food system is a complex international network that provides ease and convenience, but at a cost. The growing disconnect between food producers, their product and consumers has caused health issues, environmental problems, human injustices and a lack of knowledge and closeness with the environment from which we live off. Organic farming, sustainable agriculture and the farm-to-table movement are growing in popularity as attention to the environment increases and healthy, organic, seasonal food becomes more accessible. Not only have restaurants began to embrace these ideas, and farmer's markets become more popular, but organizations like WWOOF have given people the opportunity to reeducate their communities and become reconnected and directly involved with the production of our food.

WWOOF –What is it?

WWOOF stands for Willing Workers on Organic Farms, but is now more commonly known as World Wide Opportunities on Organic Farms. WWOOF is a network of international organizations that links volunteers willing to learn and live on organic properties with host farms seeking help to make a more sustainable world. Volunteers give their time and labor in exchange for education, food and housing, all while traveling the world cheaply and reconnecting with nature. The organization began in the United Kingdom in 1971 by Sue Coppard,

WWOOF: Sustainable Travel Meets Sustainable Food

cont'd

a secretary in London seeking an escape from her urban duties. When created, under the name "Working Weekends on Organic Farms", the goal was to provide city dwellers the opportunity to get involved in the organic farming movement, eventually growing into a worldwide institution with over 50 countries around the world involved. Although there is an international website, WWOOF programs operate independently within each country, giving volunteers the opportunity to focus on specific regions.

How it works?

To become a WWOOF member, depending on the country/region chosen, you can sign-up online and receive complete access to the full host directory. Each host creates a profile describing their lifestyle, location, expectations, and accommodations. Members can also create a profile describing themselves and their experience and wishes, allowing for hosts and volunteers to interact and communicate directly. Once a member has chosen their destination and host, specifications on accommodations, projects, work hours and length of stay can be discussed. Generally no money is involved as this is voluntary based, although some hosts may offer a stipend for your time and effort. Many farms vary on what they focus on, ranging from purely produce or cattle, to wineries or beekeeping, giving volunteers a wide range of options. Volunteer and host relationships are not of employee/employer but equally work together. WWOOFing is compatible with people from all walks of life, including families, groups, young, old, all are welcome. The key to a successful WWOOF job is a continuous and open communication between host and volunteer as well as an open mind and positive attitude. For more tips on how-to WWOOF: http://www.bootsnall.com/articles/12-07/the-how-tos-of-wwoofing.html

WWOOF: Sustainable Travel Meets Sustainable Food

cont'd | ## Why WWOOF?

- It gives people the rare opportunity to receive a new and valuable education while literally in the field
- A cheap and rewarding way to travel all over the world
- Get to meet all kinds of people from different cultures and backgrounds
- Potentially even earn some extra money (depending on the farm)
- Have a brand new experience outside of your comfort zone
- Improve health through diet and exercise (and maybe get a tan!)
- Learn or brush up on a new language
- Explore and reconnect with nature
- Work on environmental advocacy outside of the city for less
- Maybe even get the chance to learn a new skill unrelated to farming
- Slow down your life and relax
- If time or location permit, work while you WWOOF
- Can open new doors and opportunities to get involved or work within the industry

To learn more about WWOOFing:

http://www.wwoof.org/

http://www.wwoofinternational.org/

http://www.naturalnews.com/024818_organic_food_learning.html

http://www.guardian.co.uk/money/2011/apr/23/wwoof-world-wide-opportunities-on-organic-farms

http://beersandbeans.com/2011/03/02/the-essential-wwoofing-pack-list/

Cavallo Point – The Lodge at the Golden Gate

By Kristin Coates, Coates Consulting
May 14, 2013

Cavallo Point is an example of a successful public (National Park Service), private (Fort Baker Retreat Group LLC), and nonprofit (The Institute at the Golden Gate) partnership. This emerging trend in business is called the Fourth Sector or otherwise known as a "for-benefit" business. A Fourth Sector business or organization takes a hybrid approach that focuses on generating earned income and giving top priority to an explicit social mission. In this case study we will explore the invaluable role that each sector plays to create a sustainable tourism destination that is progressive in its business operations, protective of the environment and cultural history, and a platform for innovative ideas to flourish – personally and professionally.

Where:

Cavallo Point is located at Fort Baker, situated in Marin County at the foot of the north tower of the Golden Gate Bridge. Fort Baker lies in the heart of the Golden Gate National Recreation Area, also known as the Golden Gate National Parks (GGNP), one of the largest urban national parks in the world. Established in 1972, the Cavallo Point is located at Fort Baker, situated in Marin County at the foot of the north tower of the Golden Gate Bridge. Fort Baker lies in the heart of the Golden Gate National Recreation Area, also known as the Golden Gate National Parks (GGNP), one of the largest urban national parks in the world. Established in 1972, the GGNP has grown to more than 75,000 acres that extend from Phleger Estate in San Mateo County to Tomales Bay in Marin County. The GGNP is also one of the nation's largest coastal preserves, with 59 miles of bay and ocean shoreline, and attracts 16 million visitors each year, making it one of the country's most highly visited national parks. The park contains numerous historical,

cont'd

Cavallo Point – The Lodge at the Golden Gate

cultural, and natural resources representing centuries of history and over 1,200 plant and animal species.

History:

In 1866, the U.S. Army acquired the Fort Baker site to fortify the north side of the Golden Gate. Following World War II, the post served as an Army reserve training facility and headquarters for anti-aircraft training units defending the Bay Area. Fort Baker, which essentially took its modern shape between 1901 and 1915, was listed in 1973 as a Historic District on the National Register of Historic Places. In August 2001, the final transfer from the Army to the National Park Service was completed, including 45 acres at the heart of Fort Baker – an intact collection of over two-dozen historic military buildings dating from the turn of the century, surrounding a 10-acre parade ground.

The Plan to Protect and Preserve Fort Baker:

The National Park Service's (NPS) mission is to "preserve unimpaired the natural and cultural resources and values of the national park system for the enjoyment, education, and inspiration of this and future generations. The Park Service cooperates with partners to extend the benefits of natural and cultural resource conservation and outdoor recreation throughout this country and the world."

Unable to meet the financial needs of maintaining and preserving the acreage and historic buildings due to federal cut backs to the Department of Interior in 1999, the National Park Service released a Request for Qualifications (RFQ) for private developers and operators to preserve the historic property and operate a hospitality destination.

The RFQ stipulated "preservation of historic structures and natural features of the site through selection of compatible uses and rehabilitation, restoration and other site improvements.

Cavallo Point – The Lodge at the Golden Gate

cont'd

A retreat and conference center would be created in the historic buildings around the parade ground and in the adjacent non-historic Capehart area. A program element would be developed to create a distinct identity for the retreat and conference center and to strengthen the relationship of uses of the center's facilities to National Park purposes and the National Park mission. New compatibly designed construction would provide adequate space for meetings, dining and accommodations."

Over half a dozen groups submitted their qualifications and vision for the historic Fort Baker property. The proposal of Passport Resorts and Equity Community Builders was accepted to submit a more detailed proposal for the preservation, development, and future operations of the project for the duration of at least 65 years. Although each submission was unique in its approach, the Passport Resort submission was chosen for its credentials in developing and operating sustainable hospitality destinations, attention to service and guest experience, reduced number of rooms (hence cutting down on environmental impact and local traffic), and community relations.

Some of the highlights of the project plan included:

- Adaptive reuse of the buildings and site for minimal impact on the environment and a sense of place
- Planning and designing a place that continues to reflect the history, land, and culture
- Creating a place to convene and foster connection
- Providing access to unparalleled natural resources with high-quality guest experiences, opportunities for discovery and creativity, and an open exchange of ideas
- Collaborating with the National Park Service, National Park Service Park Partners, learning institutions, and global leaders
- Perpetuating a commitment to lifelong learning

Cavallo Point – The Lodge at the Golden Gate

cont'd

Cavallo Point opened in the summer of 2007. The property received LEED Gold accreditation for its reuse of existing buildings and green designs.

Cavallo Point – The Lodge at the Golden Gate:

Today, Cavallo Point is comprised of 142 guest lodging units of which half the units are in 11 newly constructed buildings, and include "green" features such as energy efficiency, water-saving technologies, and natural, recycled and sustainably produced finishes. All new buildings on the property were built on existing footprints of the former Capehart houses. Built in the 1960s, the Capehart houses are not of historical significance and therefore were unprotected under the National Historic Register. The other units are in 13 historic buildings that have been restored to the criteria of the National Historic Register where the historic trim, high-pressed tin ceilings, hardwood floors, and fireplaces were kept intact.

Also on the property is Murray Circle Restaurant named for horseshoe shaped road where Fort Baker resides. The Farley Bar was named for a local hero, Phil Frank. A beacon of the Sausalito community, Phil Frank was a creator of the San Francisco based comic strip, Farley, and an enthusiast of the Parks. He passed away in 2007.

Over fifteen thousand square feet of meeting and conference space in various room sizes and configurations including an historic chapel is the destination for countless corporate, social, and nonprofit meetings. Unlike many other corporate group destinations, Cavallo Point is special not only for its retreat setting so close to an international airport, but also for the little touches such as windows that open in meeting rooms, mostly organic and local food, and open space for group activity.

Cavallo Point – The Lodge at the Golden Gate

cont'd

The Healing Arts Center and Spa is comprised of approximately nine thousand square feet of new construction and over four thousand square feet in three historic buildings. The wellness program includes an Integrative Medicine Doctor, and spa treatments that use locally blended oils from the eucalyptus, bay laurel trees, and lavender that grow on or near the property.

The Cavallo Point Experience:

More and more Americans are seeking values-based experiences that foster connection, create a sense of community and place, and enrich the quality of life. Consumers are searching for more than commodities – they want experiences that will transform them and help sustain their transformation. Consumers are looking for "personal trainers for the soul."

The vision for Cavallo Point – The Lodge at the Golden Gate was to create a destination that not only appealed to the traditional market mix of the leisure traveler and group market, but also to be a destination for lifelong learning. Being located in the center of a national park rich with outdoor recreation and discovery, and only minutes from one of the world's most sophisticated metropolitan cities, San Francisco, opportunities for cultural immersion, the arts, and innovation are abundant. Cavallo Point was designed to be both a destination for visitors coming from afar and a regular meeting place for locals. This balance is a key to success of any sustainable tourism destination. Given that the Bay Area is a nationally recognized destination for the organic food movement, the healing arts, visual arts, and recreation, programs were designed for guests to participate in multiple day, immersion retreats led by well-known talent. Other

Cavallo Point – The Lodge at the Golden Gate

cont'd

touch points that illustrated this commitment to lifelong learning and celebrating the local culture included:

- An extensive visual arts program seen throughout the property including an art gallery, photography in all the guest rooms and public spaces, and outdoor sculpture
- A wine cellar with local, cult wines of the region and from afar
- A cooking school offering evening classes, group experiences, and multiple day classes
- Free daily yoga, weekend guided hikes, and history tours of the property
- A mercantile and healing arts boutique that sells products made by local artisans and with an environmental ethic

The common threads that weave their way through the guest experience are a high level of guest services, a deep connection to the landscape, a lasting relationship with the community and staff, and a feeling of contentment that keeps guests returning time after time. The experience is defined by authenticity; spaces are designed to reflect the landscape and the culture, and incorporate sensual and subtle details. It is also defined by deep comfort.

The Development Team:

The Fort Baker Retreat Group is comprised of Passport Resorts and Equity Community Builders, working with the National Park Service and an award-winning design team to develop a project that most efficiently and elegantly utilizes the site to create a one-of-a-kind retreat environment.

Passport Resorts is known for developing and operating destination resorts that promote environmental responsibility and sustainable development while offering a luxurious and soulful guest experience. Passport is the management company

Cavallo Point – The Lodge at the Golden Gate

cont'd

that operates the internationally acclaimed Post Ranch Inn, and formerly the Jean-Michel Cousteau Fiji Islands Resort and Hotel Hana-Maui. All their current and past projects share a reverence for the land, community, and local culture. Equity Community Builders LLC (ECB) is a San Francisco-based real estate developer and project manager that specializes in in-fill residential, commercial, and historic rehabilitation projects in northern California. ECB has completed and manages more than $400 million-worth of development for its own account, in partnerships, or for clients under management agreements. ECB is recognized for its economically sound and award-winning development projects and expertise in military base adaptive reuse, historic rehabilitation, ground leases, and sustainable design and development practices. ECB is best known for its many projects in the Presidio of San Francisco, including the Thoreau Center for Sustainability, Building 38, and The Bay School. ECB has a long-standing relationship with both the National Park Service and its nonprofit partner, the Golden Gate National Parks Conservancy. Since 1994, ECB has negotiated four long-term leases with the NPS and its affiliate, the Presidio Trust, involving 14 buildings with over 275,000 square feet of major historic rehabilitation projects.

The Institute at the Golden Gate

A program of the Golden Gate National Parks Conservancy in partnership with the National Park Service, the Institute at the Golden Gate is an on-site, non-profit organization that fosters new ideas, shares best practices, encourages leadership, and supports and implements public policy changes that will benefit people and the planet. The Institute is currently focused on how parks can connect to people's health, sustainable food systems, and climate change education. Since its launch in 2008, the Institute has helped shape national food policy and is implementing the groundbreaking "Healthy Parks Healthy

Cavallo Point – The Lodge at the Golden Gate

cont'd

People" initiative in the U.S. As they enter their fifth year, the Institute is building on its early successes and launching into a broader range of programmatic activities to bring about real change. In addition to its health, food and climate education programs, in 2013 the Institute will be launching a fourth program on urban areas and a fellowship for emerging environmental leaders. Ten percent of all room nights at the retreat are available at the federal per diem rate for attendees of the Institute programs, conferences, and workshops.

Cavallo Point in 2013:

As with any new hospitality destination, it takes a minimum of three years to generate revenue and build occupancy. Cavallo Point was no different, and beat the odds given that the property opened in one of the country's largest recessions. Today, Cavallo Point is a thriving and cherished local hangout, and a national and international travel destination. The management is always striving to raise the bar on environmental stewardship, creating a one-of-a-kind guest experience, and leading the way in progressive hospitality. Travelers expect more today and are motivated by their values and the authenticity of service, style, and experience. That "X-Factor" can be witnessed at Cavallo Point and is the result of a hybrid approach.

Kristin Coates is the principal of Coates Consulting

LOS POBLANOS HISTORIC INN & ORGANIC FARM

Los Ranchos, New Mexico, USA

www.lospoblanos.com

Photo courtesy of Dean Houghton.

For an intimate land-based stay in the heart of New Mexico, Los Poblanos tops the list. This ecotourism destination combines lodging, a working organic farm, a lavender business, and farm-to-table restaurant, all under the same uniting mission to "celebrate and educate about high-quality land-based lifestyles."

Environmental stewardship is embodied in a number of ways at Los Poblanos. Most notably, the inn is dedicated to the preservation of the region's agricultural history. This is reflected in the large portion of land designated as an organic farm that grows many heirloom and native varieties of produce to supply the inn's kitchen as well as local CSAs (Community Supported Agriculture). Amongst the New Mexico staples, beets, carrots, radicchio, lettuce, onions, mâche, kale, spinach, fava beans, Chimayo chiles, o'odham cowpeas, casaba melons, brown tepary beans and magdelena big cheese squash make up just a handful of the delightful bounty. The farmers utilize organic and local agricultural methods that respect the land and provide nutrient-rich, delicious local produce year-round.

To foster this spirit of preservation in others, Los Poblanos has instated a volunteer program to work with students and community members interested in learning about organic farming, eco-hospitality, and sustainable business. Individuals are invited to work with the inn and its farm to learn the daily tasks and responsibilities involved in running a successful eco business. By proxy, if not consciously, volunteers are exposed to the core values that drive Los Poblanos to excel, including a respect for nature, an understanding of the value of history, and a desire to educate the public.

Los Poblanos is deeply connected to the local community and surrounding region. In addition to the inn's direct efforts to preserve native agriculture through its organic farm, the inn also supports other groups and organization dedicated to conservation, preservation, and environmental and cultural education efforts locally. Los Poblanos also hosts events to support and raise money for local schools, farming, local food groups, historic preservation, museums, economic development and local tourism groups, various departments at the University of New Mexico, and the Albuquerque Convention and Visitors Bureau. The inn's ties to the land have naturally extended into efforts to support education and cultural preservation in the local community.

By offering educational and cultural programs, promoting local plant and wildlife preservations, offering volunteer opportunities on their organic farm and gardens, and supporting local organizations, Los Poblanos Inn has become a leader in environmental stewardship.

LAPA RIOS

Osa Peninsula, Costa Rica

www.laparios.com

Photo courtesy of Lapa Rios

The Lapa Rios Ecolodge and Wildlife Preserve operates on the belief that no matter how you cut it, a rainforest left standing is worth more. Located in Costa Rica in the private Lapa Rios Reserve on the Osa Peninsula, the resort preserves its idyllic scenery by employing extraordinary business practices that support environmental preservation and conservation.

Despite being perched in the middle of the rainforest, no live trees were cut for the construction of its sixteen private bungalows. Lapa Rios takes a strong stand against cutting down the rainforest by reporting any illegal logging activities to the local authorities and the press and refusing to cut the rainforest canopy above nearby roads (contrary to local law) in order to preserve "monkey bridges." The resort even encourages guests to participate in their preservation efforts by offering a Volunteer Reforestation Program, whereby guests transplant a primary rain forest seedling to an area of secondary growth, all while learning about the specific tree and its role in the ecosystem. In an effort to preserve and conserve the 1000-acre nature reserve, access to its interior is only permitted if accompanied by a professional guide.

Lapa Rios provides an ecotourism opportunity that emphasizes environmental and intercultural education for both visitors and local residents. Its efforts to protect and preserve the surrounding rainforest and local beaches and foster a learning experience for tourists have resulted in positive impacts on the local region.

5

Developing an Ecotourism Business Plan

AN INTUITIVE STARTING POINT WHEN BUILDING A NEW BUSINESS IS to define your mission statement. Once your mission statement is sufficiently identified and described, the rest of the business will be built to support and uphold this mission. As a sustainability-oriented entrepreneur, your mission may include either or both local conservation and community development. It is important to support these goals with strong business models in order to optimize your chances of success.

A detailed and focused business plan will not only help you to align your actions with your end goal, but it will also give you a checklist to help motivate you to take the next steps and keep moving forward. There are a vast number of templates to choose from when it comes to business plans. A structured business plan will include the following:

- A brief description of your business model: Describe the product (and production method) or service—what sets you apart in the existing market? Where will your business be located? How will people get to and from your business?

- Organizational Overview: What will the organizational structure be? What will your management system be? How many staff will be required? What type of skills and background will your staff need? How will you attract the right people (consider training, benefits, competitive wages)?

- A brief description of the ideal customer: Where will demand for your product/service come from? Research relevant customer demographics.

- An overview and analysis of current and potential competitors: What is their product or service? How is it similar or different from yours? How are they running their business? What tools and platforms are they using (Customer Relationship Management systems, social media platforms, donations platforms, partners, etc)?

- An overview and analysis of current and potential partners: Are there existing like-minded organizations? What other local or non-local businesses would make a good partner?

- An analysis of finances: How much investment will be required to launch this business? How will the business be financed—equity, private loans, conventional financing venues such as banks and credit unions, government agencies? Be sure to consider financing options that provide incentives or development aid to businesses implementing green practices. Once the business is established, what are the operation costs? What is the anticipated income? How long will it take to break even, to make a profit? How will you determine the price of your product or service?

Starting a business involves many legal considerations. For most entrepreneurs, this is outside of the realm of their expertise. When it comes to legal structure and names; tax responsibilities; federal, city, and county requirements; and analyzing finances, seek out advice and guidance from the respective professionals. This will ensure that you have full and accurate information to help guide your decisions.

Ecotourist Market Description

Definitive, current studies of ecotourists are hard to come by. Taking this into account, the following overview is based on several WTO and IUCN studies and the direct observations of the authors and contributors to this book.

Tourism Queenland (www.tq.com.au) has conducted some interesting surveys using the following definition of ecotourism:

"For the purpose of this research, an Ecotourist is defined as someone who did at least one of the following activities on their last long haul holiday:

- Saw wildlife in its natural surroundings
- Stayed in the wilderness
- Visited a rainforest/ jungle
- Visited national parks

And agreed that they look for at least one of the following activities:

- Environmental/ ecological sites to visit
- See wildlife in natural surroundings
- Walk in untouched countryside and natural environments

And sometimes plan holidays around at least one of the following activities:

- Bird or animal watching
- Camping
- Nature/ ecological/ environmental/ wilderness/ activities
- Walking/ hiking/ bush walking/ rainforest walking/ rambling
- See wildlife in natural surrounds"

Australia in general and Queensland specifically have a very sophisticated tourism sector and of course ecotourism opportunities abound. Reports published by Tourism

cont'd

Ecotourist Market Description

Queensland examine tourist demographics from different countries. These reports conclude:

- 26% of tourists from the United Kingdom meet their definition as ecotourists
- 20% of American tourists had the same qualification
- 28% of all Chinese tourists also qualified

These numbers are far above former estimates, suggesting to us that ecotourism worldwide might account for over 10% of all tourism and climbing.

Demographic Observations

There are three major categories of ecotourists by age: youthful ecotourists between the ages of 18-30 who tend to engage in adventure travel; family groups with school-age children whose parents wish to expose them to the wonders of our planet; and mature travelers over fifty and well into the upper decades who love to travel, love nature, and have the time and means to push the envelope of exploration, especially to more costly areas.

Expenditure

"In Australia anecdotal evidence suggests the ecotourists spend up to 50% more than the average tourist and stay up to twice as long." (www.bgci.org)

Other studies also have suggested that ecotravelers may be willing to spend more money on their largely off-the-beaten-path tourism activities. This is certainly the case for other groups involved in experiential travel.

This chapter also appears in "IUCN Best Practice Guidelines on Sustainable Tourism in Protected Areas."

6

Ecotourism Marketing Basics

AFTER PUTTING SO MUCH EFFORT AND PLANNING INTO THE creation of a new business or the improvement of an existing business, how do you get your message out to the public, and more importantly, how do you reach the right audience? The following is an overview of several common promotional outlets.

WEB-BASED MARKETING

It is no longer a secret that most travelers prepare for a trip using the internet. This makes it critical for your business to be well-represented and easily found in cyber space. According to a survey conducted in 2009 by E-Marketer, Barlow Researchers, U.S. Census Bureau, and Jupiter Research (3.15.2012), nearly 60% of small businesses either had a website or were planning to get a website. Although having a website in today's internet-savvy world is critical, it is no longer sufficient. Businesses are increasing their web presence by engaging in social media, joining online directories, and sometimes even investing in paid search advertising. Here are the basics to get your business up-to-date on the world wide web.

Website

Most important is creating a pleasant experience for visitors who come to your website for information. Your website is very likely one of the first places that a potential customer will learn about you. There is no need to emphasize how important first impressions can be. This is not the time for a sales pitch, but rather, this is your opportunity to provide quality information and initiate a positive relationship. The top qualities of a successful website include providing keyword rich and relevant content, attractive structure that allows for easy navigation, and regular maintenance to keep it looking fresh and unique.

Your website content is your means to communicate with visitors on the web. Be sure to offer relevant information and keep your content typo-free. Content is the #1 means to increase your website's performance in the search engines. It may be time consuming, but it is well worth the investment. Creating content that reaffirms what you offer and why you matter in your specific niche is not only helpful to your potential customers and clients, it confirms to the search engines that your website is credible and relevant.

Be sure to have a clear vision and understanding of your intended message before you begin writing content or designing your website. This will assist in developing a natural structure for your website. One of the first questions to ask is how many pages will your website require today, and what pages might you need to develop in the future? Designing a navigation structure that is easy to use and leaves room for future growth is critical in ensuring a pleasant visitor experience.

Give your visitors a reason to come back to your website. If your website remains static for all time, there is little incentive for return visits. Provide seasonal content and images to keep repeat visitors interested and engaged. Provide a blog, a newsfeed, a sign-up form for your e-newsletter, a white paper library—the possibilities are endless.

If your business doesn't have a website yet, consider a low cost option such as a website builder. There are a growing number of free website builders available, such as Drupal, Joomla, Wordpress, etc. These templatized programs make it a breeze to build and manage your own website with very little knowledge of html.

Social Media

What may have begun as a way to keep a tab on long-lost friends and distant relatives has evolved into a noteworthy marketing tool. Social media has exploded in the last two years and has become an integral part of corporate marketing strategies. Is it worth your attention? In short, yes.

True, participating in social media platforms increases your online presence, which is noted by search engines and helps to improve your search engine performance. More importantly, social media gives businesses a human voice. It allows you to make your brand come alive, which allows your customers and clients to identify with you and encourages them to follow you—which ultimately leads to sales and increased revenue for you.

There is no need to be intimidated by social media. With these five best practices in mind, businesses can reap the benefits and cultivate positive relationships, without the headache.

Before you create a presence on any social media platform, be sure to outline clear editorial guidelines. Decide which topics are appropriate to discuss and engage in, and which ones should be avoided at all costs. This is the simplest way to ensure that your social media presence stays focused on your product or service and maintains relevant and informative conversations.

Anticipate and prepare for a crisis. When interacting with humans, negative comments are unavoidable. This is just the simple result of it not being feasible to please everyone. However, you should have a predetermined method of handling these less-than-optimal interactions. Do you address the negative comment by following it with a positive resolution? Do you remove it altogether? Do you encourage interaction from other followers? Whatever your decision, preparing for crisis allows for an organized and well-thought response when the time comes.

Engage with your followers. As with any relationship, one must give and take to maintain a healthy dynamic. This involves listening and staying in-tune with your followers' interests and current concerns. It's not enough to post once and then turn your back. It is important to follow a conversation and respond, offer tips or helpful resources when someone asks a question, share an opinion, etc.

Stay tuned. Social media can't be turned off when other tasks take priority. Whether or not you are monitoring your accounts, your followers will be interacting with you. The more responsive you are, the better your relationship will be. This may mean beginning with just one or two social media platforms in order to ensure that enough time is devoted to each. It's better to have fewer, well-managed accounts than a multitude of abandoned accounts.

Use tools to save time and energy. Nowadays, there are a variety of tools to help you manage multiple social media accounts from one platform. These tools not only enable you to post to multiple accounts simultaneously, they also provide you with helpful statistics to gauge your performance. If you are ready to tackle multiple social media channels, be sure to check out Hootsuite, SocialOoph, and SproutSocial.

Online Directories

Online directories can be a web searcher's best friend. These aggregate sites provide a tailored list of businesses with the click of a button—and all are relevant and on-point with the web searcher's query. Although not all industries have useful online directories, be sure to do your research and see if your business could be added to an existing directory.

Most useful directories will show up amongst the first search engine results for their targeted search phrase. This is usually because they are well-established and have built a strong reputation in the search engines. If your business is listed in a directory, you increase your chances of being found on the web. Also, having a direct link from this well-established directory to your independent website helps to reaffirm to the search engines that your website is relevant, which helps improve your search engine performance.

Paid Search Advertising

The beauty of paid search advertising comes in its flexibility. With the ability to test large volumes of keywords and receive speedy feedback, it's easy to make adjustments and optimize your ads and keywords in a relatively short time frame. You choose your budget, you choose your keywords, and in return, you receive quality traffic.

Paid search advertising has a very low upfront cost. Setting up an account is free of charge (other than the time it will take to create it). Advertisers have two options: pay each time someone clicks on an ad (great for driving traffic to a certain page), or pay each time an ad is displayed (great for increasing brand awareness). In either case, you decide the highest bid you are willing to pay for any keyword, and your set your maximum daily budget. You have the option to start small until you become familiar with the tools and processes, and then go as big as you like. The most important cautionary note is to monitor your account often, as paid search advertising has the potential to blow through a lot of cash quickly if you are not disciplined and experienced in this kind of marketing.

In designing your paid search advertising campaign, you will be able to drill down on very specific keywords and target a very specific demographic. Paid search advertising allows you to cater to each specific niche of your market on an intimate level, a feature that is not available through organic search campaigns. Instead of focusing on your top three to five driving keywords as you would when developing content for your website, paid search advertising allows you to tap into Pandora's box and explore hundreds or thousands of keywords. This enables you to have extremely targeted promotions, such as seasonal offers, geo-specific ads, or product-specific ads.

Despite its many advantages, paid search advertising is not for everyone. It lends itself very naturally to product-based ecommerce sites, but it may be more difficult for a service-based site to measure viability. Without a financial value to associate to each click, how can you determine a cost-effective bid? Despite this limitation, paid search advertising can be quite successful, even under small marketing budgets, in acquiring new customers, generating new leads, and making direct sales.

PRINT MARKETING

Do not be fooled by the internet revolution and the tidal technology wave. Print is still alive and well and should absolutely hold a place in your marketing strategy. Print materials such as brochures, leaflets, flyers, and even the old-fashioned business card are great collaterals to give away at tradeshows, information tables, and other live events.

Newspapers and magazines, although decreasing in circulation, are still quite popular. Consider purchasing ad space in a niche newspaper or magazine that speaks directly to your target audience.

There is also the possibility of creating your own print publication, especially if you can offer readers pertinent, informative content on a regular basis- perhaps a toolkit or a helpful resource.

WORD OF MOUTH

Word of mouth recommendations can be a very valuable promotion tool. To ensure that each visitor positively reviews the accommodation and their experience, formal training should be provided to all staff at the accommodation. Every staff member should have an accurate information base that includes an understanding of eco-tourism, information about conservation efforts at the facility, local attractions, and a general knowledge about the natural and cultural environment of the local area. Additionally, every employee should possess basic skills such as listening, problem-solving, providing directions, and general customer service. Finally, staff members should recognize that it is the extras that make a difference and keep visitors returning. This involves exuding respect and admiration for the area and sharing knowledge of local culture, mythology, farming, and art. It is special attention to details such as this that makes visitors feel a unique connection to the area that they visit and encourages them to share their experiences with friends, family, and the online community.

The Importance of Hospitality

You don't have to own a lodging establishment to incorporate hospitality into your everyday business. When it comes to establishing strong relationships with customers and fostering repeat business, hospitality plays a large role.

The word hospitality first appeared in the English language in the 14th century, and hospitable as an adjective first appeared circa 1570. It is defined as:

1. given to generous and cordial reception of guests

2. promising or suggesting generous and cordial welcome

3. offering a pleasant or sustaining environment

4. kindness in welcoming guests or strangers

One of the easiest ways to differentiate your business from your competitors is to welcome all visitors warmly and provide them with your own special brand of hospitality. In a world where days are crammed with too much to do and too little time to do it in, providing quality service can really make a difference in your visitor's day—which can go a long way in word-of-mouth marketing.

Hospitality is a cherished tradition throughout cultures worldwide and is perhaps summed up by one of my favorite quotes: "Don't forget to entertain strangers, for by doing so some have unknowingly entertained angels."

CREATING PARTNERSHIPS

In an effort to create partnerships with surrounding businesses and increase visitor flow, enterprises with similar values should join together to benefit each other. For example, "the owner of a hotel or other accommodation could work with a bicycle rental company to create a joint promotional package, in order to attract visitors interested in combing the two." Business partnerships such as this not only increase trust among local stakeholders, but also create a network of local resources and eco-cultural activities for visitors to take advantage of. These connections allow visitors to experience more at their destination at a lower cost, ultimately raising their overall satisfaction and encouraging them to promote your business.

Promoting Local Art

It is also common for tourism businesses to promote local artists and craftspeople by featuring their work throughout their establishment. Local artwork are popular take-home souvenirs and offering them for sale in your business helps support local artists and craftspeople. For the ultimate authentic experience, encourage the artist to sell directly to the tourist.

Conclusion

'N A WORLD WITH LIMITED RESOURCES AND A GROWING
population, nothing is more important than an environmentally mindful approach to business. Ecotourism offers a way to directly make a positive change by supporting the environment and the local population. More importantly, ecotourism has a limitless potential to indirectly lead to positive change by increasing awareness and fostering positive lifestyle changes in the visitors, staff, and local community that are involved in the business operation.

Now equipped with the building blocks of a successful ecotourism business, our wish for you is to become an active agent of positive change in your local community and the global community.

Eco Products Suggestions

Sustainable Furniture

Green Edge Supply

http://www.greenedgesupply.com/

Vaughan-Bassett

http://www.vaughan-bassett.com/

Copeland Furniture

http://www.copelandfurniture.com/

Lee

http://www.leeindustries.com/

Guild Master

http://www.guildmaster.com/

Mitchell Gold + Bob Williams

http://www.mgbwhome.com/

Selamat Designs

http://selamatdesigns.com/

Harden

http://www.hardenfurniture.com/

DuPont: Sorona Carpet

www2.dupont.com/biosciences/en-us/sorona/dupont-sorona-for-sustainable-carpet.html

Environmentally Friendly Bedding

Alpaca Culture

http://alpacaculture.com/

Coyuchi

http://www.coyuchi.com/

Cozy Pure

http://www.cozypure.com/

Ecosus Sleep Systems

http://www.ecosussleepsystems.com/

Holy Lamb Organics

http://www.holylamborganics.com/

Magniflex

http://www.magniflex.com/

Organic Mattresses

http://www.organicmattressshop.com/

Simmons

http://www.simmons.com/natural-care-bed

The Wool Bed Company

http://www.surroundewe.com/

Yala

http://www.yaladesigns.com/

Eco Friendly Cleaning Supplies

Bon Ami

http://www.bonami.com/

Caldrea

http://www.caldrea.com/

Citrus Magic

http://citrusmagic.beaumontproducts.com/

Eco-Me

http://www.eco-me.com/

Ecover

http://www.ecover.com/us

Green Works

http://www.greenworkscleaners.com/products/

J.R. Watkins

http://www.jrwatkins.com/

Method.

http://methodhome.com/

Mrs. Meyers

http://www.mrsmeyers.com/

Low-Footprint Transportation

Airnimal

http://www.airnimal.eu/

Aixam-Mega Group

www.aixam.com

EcEcoVelo

http://www.ecovelo.info/

FuelVapor Technologies, Inc.

www.fuelvapour.com

Piaggio Ape

www.piaggio.com

Planet Bike

http://www.planetbike.com/page/

Solar Sailor Holdings Ltd.

www.solarsailor.com

ZiPee

www.zipeebikes.com

Waste Management

BuildWorks

http://www.buildworks.com/airfloor/index.php

The Composting Toilet Store

http://www.composting-toilet-store.com/

Envirolet

http://www.envirolet.com/

Nature's Head

http://natureshead.net/

Santec Corporation

http://www.santeccorporation.com/

Waterless

http://www.waterless.com/

Solar Products

Sun Oven

http://www.sunoven.com/

Real Goods

http://realgoods.com/

Siemen's Solar

http://www.siemenssolar.com/

Building Materials

Homasote

http://www.homasote.com/

James Hardie

http://www.jameshardie.com/main.shtml

Louisiana-Pacific Building Products

http://www.lpcorp.com/

Low E

http://www.low-e.com/

Maze Nails

http://www.mazenails.com/

Trex

http://www.trex.com/

Weyerhaeuser

http://www.woodbywy.com/trus-joist/

Appliances

Sun Frost

http://www.sunfrost.com/

Sustainable Building Styles and Materials

Indonesia: Bamboo Sheds Image as Poor Man's Timber, Kadek Ariyani, Agence-France Presse, July 14, 2012

How to Build Green, www.greenspacencr.org

Tiny Prefab Units Promote Eco-Friendly Building, Robert Selna, May 18, 2010

House of Bamboo, Laura Sevier, April 1, 2007

David Hertz Architects & SEA Studio of Environmental Architecture, www.studioea.com

Andreas Stavropoulos, XS Land Architects, xs-land.com

Tiny Homes: Simple Shelters, Lloyd Kahn, 2012

Cob Buildings - www.cobcottage.com

Living Homes: Sustainable Architecture and Design, in Eco-friendly Homes, March 10, 2009

About Eco Tourism and Green Business

A Green Model for Eco-Tourism, World Business Council for Sustainable Development, 2005

Adapting to Climate Change and Climate Policy: Progress, Problems and Potentials, Daniel Scott and Susanne Becken, April 8, 2010

Keeping Tourism in Balance with Nature, Eifion Rees, January 5, 2010

Tourism-Led Poverty Reduction Programme, International Trade Centre, March 2009

Benefits of Becoming a Sustainable Business, www.eco-officiency.com

ECOpreneuring: Putting Purpose and the Planet before Profits, Lisa Kivirist and John Ivanko, July, 2008

Carbon Offsets

www.carbonfund.org

www.carbonoffsets.org

www.carbonneutral.com.au

www.carbonneutral.com

Transportation

Driving Growth: How Clean Cars and Climate Policy Can Create Jobs, Alan Baum and Daniel Luria, March 2010

Biofuel Benefits Go Beyond Environment, Oxford Analytics, April 4, 2006

5 Ways to Stop the Excuses & Make Eco-friendly Travel Easy, Zoë Smith, June 21st, 2012

Energy

Solar is the Solution, Steve Heckeroth, January 2008 2010

How Does Solar Energy Work, Benefits-of-Recycling, 2010

Windpowerfacts.info

Geothermal Energy—A Solid Alternate Energy Source, www.alternate-energy-sources.com

Waste Management

Environmental Benefits, Composting, www.epa.gov

GREYWATER: What It Is . . . How To Treat It . . . How To Use It, Carl Lindstrom, 2000

www.compostingtoilet.org/

http://www.brownfieldsnet.org/

Food

The Benefits of Growing Your Own Food, Liza Barnes and Nicole Nichols

CityFruit.org

Farmstead Chef, Lisa Kivirist and John Ivanko, 2011

Food Facts: the environmental impact of agriculture and food production, Sierra Club

Environmentally Friendly Food Choices, ygoy.com, August 18, 2010

10 Tips for an Eco-Friendly Meal, Don't overlook the foods you eat when it comes to going green, Jen Laskey, April 10, 2008.

CPSIA information can be obtained at www.ICGtesting.com
Printed in the USA
LVOW08s1836270814

401204LV00018B/1171/P

9 781489 542236